Old English for Young Readers:
A Brief Dictionary of KJV Biblical Terms

REBECCA IRVINE

Published by Chetnole House Publishing, LLC
Mesa, Arizona

Copyright © 2023 Rebecca Irvine
All rights reserved. No part of this book may be reproduced in any form or by any means without prior permission of the publisher, except in case of brief passages embodied in reviews and articles.

Paperback edition
Interior design by Rebecca Irvine
Interior artwork generated from public domain works by various artists
Cover art by Jeffry Byrd
Cover design by Rebecca Irvine

ISBN 978-1-7323747-4-4

For Ellie,
and the grandparents
who love her dearly.

Author's Notes

This dictionary in no way is meant to be a comprehensive listing of all the words included in the King James Version of the Bible. The over 600 words included here are those that the author considered more challenging for young readers to understand due to changes in modern English and cultural differences. These words also tend to be those that are repeated more frequently in the text. Those who would like to propose words to add to a future edition of the Old English for Young Readers can message the author on Facebook (@Rebecca Irvine). Any suggestions would be welcomed!

Additionally, an apology to all the linguists, etymologists, and word nerds out there. Yes, the use of "Old English" in the title of this little book is technically inaccurate. The KJV Bible is written in Early Modern English, not Old English. I hope you will forgive my imprecision and simply enjoy the title as an exercise in contrasting parallel structure.

Understanding the KJV Bible

In the early 1600s printing technology was just getting started. When King James took the throne in 1603, there were disagreements between different denominations about which Bible translation was the most accurate. In the Anglican church, leaders read from the Bishops Bible. However, those who were Protestant reformers relied on the Geneva Bible. The arguments between denominations were strong enough to cause concern for the monarch. King James soon approved a new translation using the nation's best theologians and scholars. He hoped it would put an end to religious strife among the people.

The translation process took seven years to complete and relied heavily on William Tyndale's original English translation (completed in 1525). In the new version, the Old Testament was translated from Hebrew, while the New Testament was translated from Greek.

When the King James Version (KJV) of the Bible was published in 1611 the English Renaissance was at its high point and Middle English was evolving. The influence of this new translation was widespread. The KJV Bible was read, heard, and studied by many and its linguistic style greatly influenced and solidified the syntax and style of the English language.

The KJV Bible became a celebrated piece of literature, rivaling the most popular writings of the day. And over the ensuing centuries, the works of many great orators, authors, and artists were inspired by the stories, poetry, and language found in the KJV. Its legacy has been widespread and enduring.

Different Spellings and Word Structures

The KJV Bible was published during a time when English spelling had not yet been standardized. At the time, there was no official body regulating the English language, and spelling varied widely between regions and even individual speakers.

The translators of the KJV Bible were instructed to use the spelling conventions of their day, which included many words and spellings that by modern day standards are considered archaic or obsolete. For example, the letter "u" was often used in place of "v," and the letter "j" was not yet commonly used.

Additionally, the KJV Bible was based on earlier English translations of the Bible, such as the Tyndale Bible and the Geneva Bible, which had their own distinctive spellings and language. The translators of the KJV Bible were instructed to retain much of the language of these earlier translations, including their spellings, in order to maintain continuity with the English Bible tradition.

Words Ending in -Eth

Readers of the KJV Bible might notice there are a lot of words in it that end with -eth. This is because when the Bible was first translated into English, there were two additional letters of the alphabet called *eth* and *thorn*.

The letter eth looked somewhat like a crossed lowercase d, like this: ð. And the letter thorn looked like this: þ. Both eth and thorn represented 'th' sounds in words but varied depending on the accents placed on sounds and syllables.

At the time of the translation process, both eth and thorn were commonly used in English. As a result, many words in the KJV Bible translation were spelled using these two letters.

But languages change over time. In the last 400 years, because of the similarity of sounds in various dialects, the letters eth and thorn were gradually phased out. First, eth was dropped in favor of thorn. Later, thorn was also abandoned. As a result, more modern translations of the Bible do not include the Middle English -eth endings.

The letter eth, in particular, was most often used as a word ending for verbs. It was used to form the third-person singular present indicative of verbs. A good example of this is when we read "the Lord giveth" (see Job 1:21). There are some linguists who believe that verbs written with the -eth suffix in Old English were verbally pronounced as if they ended in 's,' which was a common dialectic feature before it became accepted in writing. As a result, some modern translations of Job 1:21 now read "the Lord gives".

Despite the loss of eth and thorn, the pronunciation of eth is still used in modern English to create ordinal numbers from cardinal numbers ending in -y, namely the multiples of ten: twentieth, thirtieth, etc.

Words Ending in -Est and -Eth

It is also helpful to know that the -eth and -est word endings that are so common in the KJV Bible are closely linked to the original translation process. Both endings are considered the sharp edges of verbs. They are reflective of the Greek and Hebrew language verb endings the translators found in the original texts. The -est ending indicates the singular second person (thou lovest), while the -eth ending shows third person (he, she, it loveth). The endings are a part of the primary meaning as written by the authors in Greek and Hebrew. The translators directly conveyed these tenses into English in this manner.

Abase: To lower yourself or feel less important. For example, when you make a mistake and have to admit it, or when you feel embarrassed or ashamed about something you did.

"And those that walk in pride he is able to abase [humble]" (Daniel 4:37).

Abhor: To really, really dislike something or someone, almost to the point of hating it or them. It's like when you have a negative feeling towards something, and you want nothing to do with it.

"Do not abhor [hate] us, for thy name's sake" (Jeremiah 14:21).

Abide: To stay with something or someone, even if it's difficult or challenging. For instance, when you follow a rule, even if you don't agree with it, or when you stay patient and endure a hard situation.

"And when Jesus came to the place, he looked up, and saw him, and said unto him, Zacchæus, make haste, and come down; for to day I must abide [stay] at thy house" (Luke 19:5).

Abominable: Really, really unpleasant or disgusting. It's like when something is so bad that it's almost unbearable, and it makes you feel strong dislike or disgust.

"Thou shalt not eat any abominable [sinful] thing" (Deuteronomy 14:3).

Accursed: Cursed or condemned, often associated with something or someone that is believed to bring bad luck or be evil. For example, when something is thought to have a curse on it, and people believe it is unlucky or brings harm.

"And ye, in any wise keep yourselves from the accursed [cursed] thing, lest ye make yourselves accursed [damned]" (Joshua 6:18).

Adjure: To seriously or solemnly ask or command someone to do something. Such as when someone, usually in a position of authority, gives a strong and urgent request or command.

"What have I to do with thee, Jesus, thou Son of the most high God? I adjure [swear to] thee by God, that thou torment me not" (Mark 5:7).

Admonish: To firmly scold or warn someone when they have done something wrong or made a mistake. It's like when someone, usually a parent or teacher gives a strong and serious warning.

"Yet count him not as an enemy, but admonish [encourage] him as a brother" (2 Thessalonians 3:15).

Adultery: When a person who is married engages in a romantic or sexual relationship with someone who is not their husband or wife. For example, when someone who is married cheats on their spouse.

"Thou shalt not commit adultery [break marriage vows]" (Exodus 20:14).

Adversary: someone or something that opposes or goes against you. It's like an opponent or an enemy. An adversary can be a person, a group of people, or even a challenging situation. In the Bible it is often a reference to Satan.

"Because your adversary [enemy] the devil, as a roaring lion, walketh about, seeking whom he may devour" (1 Peter 5:8).

Adversity: when you face difficult or challenging situations or circumstances that can make things tough for you. For example, facing obstacles, setbacks, or hardships that can make life hard or uncomfortable.

"In the day of prosperity be joyful, but in the day of adversity [hardship] consider: God also hath set the one over against the other" (Ecclesiastes 7:14).

Afflict: to cause someone or something to suffer or experience pain, distress, or discomfort. For instance, making someone go through a difficult or challenging time by persecuting them.

"Ye shall afflict [persecute] your souls, and do no work at all" (Leviticus 16:29).

Amen: a word that is often used at the end of prayers or religious expressions to express agreement or approval. It's like saying "yes" or "I agree" to show agreement or support for what has been said.

"And all the people shall answer and say, Amen [I agree]" (Deuteronomy 27:14-15).

Apostle: important messengers who spread the teachings or gospel principles. In the Bible, an apostle was a person with authority sent forth to witness of Christ and his gospel.

"And when it was day, he called unto him his disciples: and of them he chose twelve, whom also he named apostles [messengers]" (Luke 6:13).

Anon: an old-fashioned term that means "soon" or "in a short time." For example, if someone says, "I will return anon," it means they will be back soon or shortly.

"But he that received the seed into stony places, the same is he that heareth the word, and anon [soon] with joy receiveth it" (Matthew 13:20).

Armor: special clothing or gear that is worn by fighters or soldiers to protect their bodies from getting hurt during battles or fights. Also called mail, armor is a tough outer covering that helps to keep soldiers safe from harm.

"And Saul armed David with his armour [protective covering], and he put an helmet of brass upon his head; also he armed him with a coat of mail" (1 Samuel 17:38).

Ascend: a word that describes the action of rising or climbing to a higher point or level. Climbing a staircase, going up a hill, or rising to the top of a mountain are all examples of ascending.

"For thou hast said in thine heart, I will ascend [rise] into heaven" (Isaiah 14:13).

Ashamed: feeling embarrassed, guilty, or sorry about something you did or said that you know is wrong or socially unacceptable. It's like feeling bad about your actions or words and wishing you could take them back.

"And my people shall never be ashamed [embarrassed]" (Joel 2:26).

Assembly: a gathering or meeting of people who come together for a specific purpose or activity. For instance, when a group of individuals meet together in one place to work on a project goal or discuss a topic.

"I will praise the Lord with my whole heart, in the assembly [gathering] of the upright, and in the congregation" (Psalm 111:1).

Astonished: to be greatly surprised or amazed by something. For example, if you receive a surprise gift, you might be astonished.

"And it came to pass, when Jesus had ended these sayings, the people were astonished [amazed] at his doctrine" (Matthew 7:28).

Athirst: a strong craving or longing for something, similar to feeling very thirsty for water.

"Lord, when saw we thee an hungred, or athirst [thirsty]" (Matthew 25:44).

Atonement: generally, an atonement is the act of making amends for a mistake or wrongdoing. The atonement of Jesus Christ, through His death and resurrection, made amends for the mistakes of all mankind.

"And he shall make an atonement [amends] for the holy place, because of the uncleanness of the children of Israel, and because of their transgressions in all their sins" (Leviticus 16:16).

Avenge: to seek justice or retribution on behalf of oneself or others for a perceived wrongdoing or harm. If someone harms a loved one, you might feel the desire to avenge the harm by calling the police.

"For he will avenge [seek justice for] the blood of his servants, and will render vengeance to his adversaries" (Deuteronomy 32:43).

Babylon: the capital city of an ancient country called Babylonia. Babylon was known as a wicked place.

"Flee out of the midst of Babylon [a wicked place], and deliver every man his soul" (Jeremiah 51:6).

Backbiting: a behavior where someone gossips or speaks negatively about another person behind their back. If someone talks negatively about a classmate to others, making unkind comments about their appearance or abilities, that would be considered backbiting.

"The north wind driveth away rain: so doth an angry countenance a backbiting [gossiping] tongue" (Proverbs 25:23).

Backsliding: the act of reverting or losing ground from previously achieved progress or improvement, often in terms of behavior or attitude. In scriptural terms it usually refers to falling back into error or sin, like someone who had quit smoking but then started again.

"I will heal their backsliding [falling back into sin], I will love them freely" (Hosea 14:4).

Balance: a word that describes a judgement of fairness or impartiality, where different sides or opinions are given equal consideration or weight. When something is balanced it is considered fair or good.

"Let me be weighed in an even balance [judged as good], that God may know mine integrity" (Job 31:6).

Band: something used to hold things together or keep them in place (sometimes by force). For example, a rubber band is a stretchy strip of rubber used to hold objects together, and a band-aid is a small adhesive strip used to cover and protect a wound. In the Bible, sometimes bands are like chains or handcuffs on a prisoner.

"Loose thyself from the bands [chains] of thy neck, O captive daughter of Zion" (Isaiah 52:2).

Baptize: to immerse or fully submerge in water. Baptism is an ordinance people perform to show their inner commitment to Christ. Sometimes baptism is used to describe being spiritually cleansed by the Holy Spirit (baptism of "fire").

"Then cometh Jesus from Galilee to Jordan unto John, to be baptized [immersed in water] of him" (Matthew 3:13).

Barren: unable to have children or offspring. It can be used to describe a woman who is unable to conceive or carry a pregnancy to term, or an animal that is unable to have babies due to physical or biological reasons.

"But Sarai was barren [unable to have children]; she had no child" (Genesis 11:30).

Base: an old-fashioned word that means something is wicked or unrighteous. For example, a book that encourages people to hurt people, to disobey commandments, or to mock good things might be described as base.

"And base [wicked] things of the world, and things which are despised, hath God chosen, yea, and things which are not, to bring to nought things that are" (1 Corinthians 1:28).

Beam: a ceiling rafter, a post, or piece of timber. Beams are often used in construction and architecture to provide structural support to the roof of a building and to bridges.

"And why beholdest thou the mote that is in thy brother's eye, but considerest not the beam [post] that is in thine own eye?" (Matthew 7:3).

Bear: to endure or carry a burden. The past tense of bear is bore or borne. For example, a heavy load or burden can be "borne" by someone who carries it on their back, or a river can "bear" a boat downstream.

"And whosoever doth not bear [endure] his cross, and come after me, cannot be my disciple" (Luke 14:27).

Beelzebub: a devil or a demon, often associated with wickedness or temptation. In the Bible, it is sometimes used as a name for Satan. Originally, Beelzebub was a Philistine god that supposedly had power over flies.

"But when the Pharisees heard it, they said, This fellow doth not cast out devils, but by Beelzebub [Satan] the prince of the devils" (Matthew 12:24).

Begotten: born or brought into existence by parents. Begotten is the past tense of begat. When someone describes the birth of their grandfather, they might say, "A long-awaited son was begotten at last."

"For in Christ Jesus I have begotten [gave birth to] you through the gospel" (1 Corinthians 4:15).

Beguile: to deceive or trick someone using charm, cleverness, or craftiness. It can be used to describe a situation where someone uses cleverness to mislead or trick others, like when a magician uses slight of hand to perform a trick.

"Let no man beguile [deceive] you of your reward in a voluntary humility and worshipping of angels" (Colossians 2:18).

Behold: a command to look at, pay attention to, or notice something of import. For instance, if a teacher wants students to pay close attention, they could ask them to "behold the information in the textbook."

"Behold [pay attention], I stand at the door, and knock: if any man hear my voice, and open the door, I will come in to him, and will sup with him, and he with me" (Revelation 3:20).

Believe: to accept or trust something as true, even if you can't see or prove it. It involves having faith or trust in something. For example, you might believe in the existence of God, even if you can't physically see Him.

"Jesus saith unto them, Believe [trust] ye that I am able to do this?" (Matthew 9:28).

Beloved: someone or something that is held in high affection or esteem, and is greatly loved, cherished, or treasured by others. It can be used to describe a person, a pet, or even an object.

"This is my beloved [greatly loved] Son, in whom I am well pleased" (Matthew 3:17).

Bereave: the sorrowful experience of being deprived of or losing someone or something that was previously present or valued. Mourning the death of a loved one is often called bereaving or bereavement.

"So will I send upon you famine and evil beasts, and they shall bereave [mourn] thee" (Ezekiel 5:17).

Beseech: to plead, beg, or ask for something with great earnestness or urgency. For example, a child might beseech their parent for a toy they really want. Past tense: besought.

"And, behold, a man of the company cried out, saying, Master, I beseech [beg] thee, look upon my son: for he is mine only child" (Luke 9:38).

Bestow: to give or grant something to someone as a gift, honor, or favor. For instance, a teacher might bestow a special award upon a student for their achievements

"And though I bestow [give] all my goods to feed the poor, and though I give my body to be burned, and have not charity, it profiteth me nothing" (1 Corinthians 13:3).

Betroth: to marry, or to promise to marry or become engaged to someone. After a couple gets engaged, they might be described as betrothed.

"And I will betroth [marry] thee unto me for ever; yea, I will betroth [marry] thee unto me in righteousness" (Hosea 2:19).

Bid: to command, order, or tell someone to do something. A parent might bid their child to go to bed early. Past tense: bade.

"Lord, if it be thou, bid [command] me come unto thee on the water" (Matthew 14:28).

Birthright: something that a person has the right to receive or inherit simply because they were born into a particular family or lineage. For example, a royal family might have a birthright to rule a kingdom.

"As Esau, who for one morsel of meat sold his birthright [inheritance]" (Hebrews 12:16).

Bishop: a pastor or manager of a church congregation. Bishops provide spiritual guidance and support to their congregations. In the Bible, a bishop is listed as being an office in the priesthood.

"If a man desire the office of a bishop [pastor], he desireth a good work" (1 Timothy 3:1).

Bitter: a taste that is sharp, unpleasant, and not sweet. Some people say the taste of medicine can be bitter on their tongue. In the Bible, the word bitter is sometimes also used to mean angry.

"Strong drink shall be bitter [unpleasant] to them that drink it" (Isaiah 24:9).

Blameless: someone or something is not at fault, guilty, or sin. A baby who does not fully understand the difference between right and wrong might be described as blameless.

"For a bishop must be blameless [without guilt]" (Titus 1:7).

Blaspheme: to speak in a disrespectful or irreverent manner about God, religion, or sacred things. It involves using words or actions that show contempt, disrespect, or insult towards beliefs or practices of others.

"I have heard all thy blasphemies [disrespectful words] which thou hast spoken against the mountains of Israel" (Ezekiel 35:12).

Blemish: a mark, spot, or flaw that makes something look less attractive or lowers its overall quality. It can refer to physical imperfections, such as a mark on the skin or a stain on a shirt.

"But with the precious blood of Christ, as of a lamb without blemish [stain] and without spot" (1 Peter 1:19).

Bless: to ask for God's good will or generosity on someone; to speak well of, or to praise. Often in prayers people will as God to bless those who are sick or in need.

"And he said, I will not let thee go, except thou bless [ask for God's good will on] me." (Genesis 32:26).

Blindness: not able to see, either physically or spiritually. In the Bible, physical blindness sometimes is used as a symbol for spiritual blindness, or when a person refuses to see God's truths.

"That blindness [inability to see] in part is happened to Israel, until the fulness of the Gentiles be come in" (Romans 11:25).

Blood: in the Bible, blood is used in two different ways. Definition 1: martyrdom, meaning to have died for a cause. The apostle Stephen died as a martyr in the New Testament.

"The voice of thy brother's blood [martyrdom] crieth unto me from the ground" (Genesis 4:10).

Definition 2: a person should take responsibility for sin or error. For example, Christ's blood (Atonement) took responsibility for the sins of the world and made repentance possible.

"His blood [responsibility for sin] shall be upon his head, and we will be guiltless" (Joshua 2:19).

Blot Out: to cover or remove something completely, as if erasing it or making it disappear. For instance, in doing your homework, you might have to erase or blot out a mistake. In the Bible, the phrase blot out is sometimes applied to the stain of sin.

"According unto the multitude of thy tender mercies blot out [remove] my transgressions" (Psalm 51:1).

Boast: to talk or brag about yourself, or to speak with pridefulness. Teammates who won their game might boast to others about how well they played.

"Boast [brag] not thyself of to morrow; for thou knowest not what a day may bring forth" (Proverbs 27:1).

Bold: to be courageous, confident, or willing to take risks. It can describe someone who is not afraid to face challenges, who shows confidence in their actions or decisions.

Baby Moses rescued by Pharoah's daughter.

"Then Paul and Barnabas waxed bold [courageously], and said, It was necessary that the word of God should first have been spoken to you" (Acts 13:46).

Bondage: being under the control or power of someone or something else, often against one's will, like being a slave or in jail.

"And they made their lives bitter with hard bondage [slavery]" (Exodus 1:14).

Book of Life: records kept of a person's life, both earthly and heavenly. According to the Bible, the Book of Life contains the names of all those who are worthy to go to heaven.

"I will not blot out his name out of the book of life [records]" (Revelation 3:5).

Born Again: making a choice to change one's life or behavior in a positive way by adopting a new belief system or way of living. In the Bible, being born again refers to making the choice to accept Jesus as the Savior and Redeemer.

"Being born again [accepting Jesus], not of corruptible seed, but of incorruptible" (1 Peter 1:23).

Bosom: the area on the chest between the breasts. It is a common term used to describe the front part of the chest over there the heart is inside the body.

"Now there was leaning on Jesus' bosom [chest] one of his disciples, whom Jesus loved" (John 13:23).

Bowels: the organs inside the abdomen, including the stomach, intestines, and other organs involved in the digestion and elimination of food. Sometimes the word "bowels" is used in the Bible to describe where deep emotions or feelings come from in the body.

"Falling headlong, he burst asunder in the midst, and all his bowels [intestines] gushed out" (Acts 1:18).

Branch: a part of a tree that grows out from the main trunk. Symbolically, a branch is also a word used for a group of people or person, such as in a family tree.

"I will raise unto David a righteous Branch [person]" (Jeremiah 23:5).

Bread: food or sustenance for survival, either physical or spiritual. In the Bible, bread is used as a symbol for Christ. For example, during the Last Supper, Christ referred to the bread as representing His body.

"Man doth not live by bread [food] only" (Deuteronomy 8:3).

Bridegroom: a man who is either about to get married or has recently been married; a groom.
Some prophets in the Bible use bridegroom as a symbol for Jesus Christ.

"[They] took their lamps, and went forth to meet the bridegroom [groom]" (Matthew 25:1).

Bridle: a set of straps and reins that are used to harness or control a horse or other animal, particularly when riding or driving. If a cowboy wants to tame a horse, he will first need to teach it to wear a bridle so it can be controlled.

"I put my hook in thy nose, and my bridle [harness] in thy lips" (Isaiah 37:29).

Brimstone: a yellow, smelly mineral or substance that burns. In the Bible, brimstone is used to describe the fiery conditions in hell.

"He shall be tormented with fire and brimstone [hellfire]" (Revelation 14:10).

Brotherly: fraternal behavior that resembles the bond between siblings, which is usually kind, or affectionate; like brothers. If Jack treats Chris with kindness, it might be described as brotherly--even if they are not related.

"Let brotherly [fraternal] love continue" (Hebrews 13:1).

Buckler: a small, round shield used by a soldier to protect himself from blows. In a battle, a buckler might help protect a knight from being injured by a sword.

"He layeth up sound wisdom for the righteous: he is a buckler [shield] to them that walk uprightly" (Proverbs 2:7).

Byword: an old saying; something that has become proverbial and has developed deeper meaning. For example, the phrase "black sheep" has come to mean a person who is different or stands out from the rest of a group or family.

"And Israel shall be a proverb and a byword [old saying] among all people" (1 Kings 9:7).

Calf: a young animal, especially a young cow, that is not yet fully grown. It usually refers to a baby cow that is still nursing from its mother's milk.

"They have made them a molten calf [young cow], and have worshipped it" (Exodus 32:8).

Calling: an invitation from God to serve in a particular role or to fulfill a specific purpose. The prophet Jonah received a calling to be a missionary in Nineveh before he was swallowed up by the whale.

"Who hath saved us, and called us with an holy calling [invitation to serve God]" (2 Timothy 1:9).

Captain: a person who is in charge of leading and commanding a group or team. The term "captain" can be used in various contexts, such as in sports, the military, or on a ship.

"And, behold, God himself is with us for our captain [leader]" (2 Chronicles 13:12).

Captive: a person, animal, or thing that is being held against their will and unable to freely move or escape. For example, a prisoner placed in jail is considered a captive.

"Even them the king of Babylon brought captive [prisoner] to Babylon" (2 Kings 24:16).

Carcass: the body of a dead animal. A carcass may be found in nature, such as when an animal dies in the wild, or it may be intentionally produced as a result of hunting.

"And he turned aside to see the carcase [dead body] of the lion" (Judges 14:8).

Carnal: worldly, sinful, not spiritual, especially in referring to things that are related to or connected with the physical body or bodily desires.

"Who is made, not after the law of a carnal [worldly] commandment, but after the power of an endless life" (Hebrews 7:16).

Cast: to throw or discard something forcefully, often with the intention of getting rid of it or disposing of it. For example, someone may cast away trash into a garbage can or cast away old belongings during a spring cleaning.

"I beheld till the thrones were cast [thrown] down" (Daniel 7:9).

Cease: to stop or come to an end. If an activity or event is ongoing and it comes to an end, it has ceased.

"Cease [stop] to do evil" (Isaiah 1:16).

Celestial: heavenly, or of the sun. It's a word that describes things that are often seen as being high above the Earth, in the vastness of space.

"There are also celestial [heavenly] bodies" (1 Corinthians 15:40).

Centurion: a military officer in ancient Rome who oversaw 100 men. They were responsible for training the men and then leading them into battle.

"And when Jesus was entered into Capernaum, there came unto him a centurion [Roman officer]" (Matthew 8:5).

Chaff: the husk of grain, such as wheat or oats, which is discarded when the grain is harvested. It is usually dry and light, and often considered waste or undesirable because it can't be eaten or used.

"The ungodly are not so: but are like the chaff [grain husks] which the wind driveth away" (Psalm 1:4).

Charge: to give someone the responsibility or authority to be in charge of a task or group. Sometimes the person is ordered to complete the task. For instance, a coach may charge or order a team captain with the responsibility of leading the team during a game or practice.

"And he charged [ordered] them straitly that no man should know it" (Mark 5:43).

Charity: showing love; the act of showing kindness, generosity, and compassion towards those in need. The Bible teaches that Christians should strive to have deeper love and charity for all people.

"Charity [love] suffereth long, and is kind; charity envieth not; charity vaunteth not itself, is not puffed up" (1 Corinthians 13:4).

Chaste: to be pure, virtuous, or abstaining from certain behaviors, especially related to sexual activity or inappropriate behavior. A person who dresses modestly and avoids revealing clothing may be considered chaste.

"While they behold your chaste [virtuous] conversation coupled with fear" (1 Peter 3:2).

Chasten: to discipline or correct someone's behavior to improve their character. Maybe a teacher would chasten a student for misbehaving in class by giving them a warning or talking to them about their behavior.

"I will chasten [correct] him with the rod of men" (2 Samuel 7:14).

Cherub: a type of angel described as having both wings and hands and being found in the throne room of God. Cherubs are often associated with positive qualities like innocence and purity. Plural form: cherubim.

"And within the oracle he made two cherubims [angels] of olive tree" (1 Kings 6:23–28).

Christian: to be a disciple or follower of Jesus Christ. For example, Christians typically attend church services, read the Bible, pray, and strive to live according to the teachings of Jesus Christ.

"And the disciples were called Christians [followers of Christ] first in Antioch" (Acts 11:26).

Circumcise: generally, to prune or trim something back; more specifically, to remove the foreskin of the penis. In some cultures, circumcision may be practiced as a cultural tradition or as a perceived health benefit.

"Now I say that Jesus Christ was a minister of the circumcision [pruning] for the truth of God" (Romans 15:8).

Clave: The Bible uses the word clave in two different ways. Definition 1: an old-fashioned word that means grasped onto or held onto someone or something. When a grandmother holds a grandchild, it could be described as claved.

"And his soul clave [held onto] unto Dinah the daughter of Jacob, and he loved the damsel" (Genesis 34:3).

Definition 2: to split or tear apart. In an earthquake, when a fault line appears, the ground has claved apart.

"And it came to pass, as he had made an end of speaking all these words, that the ground clave [tore] asunder that was under them" (Numbers 16:31).

Comely: splendid, lovely, or attractive to look at. For example, if someone is described as "comely," it means they are seen as attractive or pleasant to look at.

"In that day shall the branch of the Lord be beautiful and glorious, and the fruit of the earth shall be excellent and comely [lovely] for them that are escaped of Israel" (Isaiah 4:2).

Comforter: another name for the Holy Ghost. When a person is stressed or feeling sad, the Holy Ghost can help them feel better and offer comfort.

"But the Comforter, which is the Holy Ghost, whom the Father will send in my name" (John 14:26).

Commend: to entrust to; to commit to the care or keeping of someone or something. For instance, if you leave to go on vacation, you might "commend" your pet to the care of a neighbor while you are gone.

"Father, into thy hands I commend [entrust] my spirit" (Luke 23:46).

Commune: to communicate or connect deeply with others, often in a personal or spiritual way. You can commune with others by sharing thoughts, feelings, or ideas in a heartfelt and meaningful way.

"And there I will meet with thee, and I will commune [communicate] with thee" (Exodus 25:22).

Compass: go in a circle or go around. Two squirrels chasing in circles around the trunk of a tree are compassing it.

"And the seventh day ye shall compass [circle around] the city seven times" (Joshua 6:4).

Conceit: a sense of vanity, prideful thoughts, or haughtiness, especially in thinking of oneself. If someone constantly brags about their achievements or looks down on others as inferior, they may be displaying conceit.

"The rich man is wise in his own conceit [vanity]" (Proverbs 28:11).

Concubine: a paramour; a woman who lives with a man as a wife, but without being married to him. In olden times, some kings or leaders would have concubines, or women who lived with them as a wife even though they weren't married.

"And David took him more concubines [paramours] and wives out of Jerusalem" (2 Samuel 5:13).

Condemnation: a strong expression of censure or disapproval, particularly from God. For example, if a pastor speaks out against an action or behavior, stating that it is morally or ethically unacceptable, they may be expressing condemnation.

"Dost not thou fear God, seeing thou art in the same condemnation [censure from God]?" (Luke 23:40).

Confess: to own up to or admit to a mistake or wrongdoing. When someone tells the truth about breaking a rule, making a mistake, or doing something wrong, they are confessing.

"I will confess [admit] his name before my Father" (Revelation 3:5).

Confirm: to make firm or strengthen through the Holy Ghost. When a person feels the Holy Ghost bear witness to truth, their testimony is confirmed.

"Who shall also confirm [strengthen] you unto the end" (1 Corinthians 1:8).

Confound: to confuse or perplex someone. For example, if a puzzle or a math problem seems very difficult to solve, it can be described as confounding.

"But God hath chosen the foolish things of the world to confound [confuse] the wise" (1 Corinthians 1:27).

Conscience: a voice inside you that gives you a sense of right and wrong. Your conscience might make you feel guilty when you do something wrong, like telling a lie or being unkind to someone.

"And they which heard it, being convicted by their own conscience [sense of right and wrong], went out one by one" (John 8:9).

Consecrate: to dedicate to God; to make something holy by promising or making a covenant. For instance, a building might be consecrated to make it a church or a temple.

"For Moses had said, Consecrate [dedicate] yourselves to day to the Lord, even every man upon his son, and upon his brother; that he may bestow upon you a blessing this day" (Exodus 32:29).

Consolation: to provide comfort, solace, or encouragement to help someone feel better. For example, if a friend is feeling sad because they lost a game, you might offer them consolation by giving them a hug.

"But woe unto you that are rich! for ye have received your consolation [comfort]" (Luke 6:24).

Constrained: being urged to do something; feeling like you have limitations or restrictions on your actions or words because of something outside of your control. When you're playing a game with specific rules that you have to follow, you might feel constrained by those rules.

"And straightway Jesus constrained [urged] his disciples to get into a ship" (Matthew 14:22).

Contention: a situation where people or groups have differing opinions or ideas and are in conflict or disagreement with each other. When two friends have different ideas about what game to play and cannot agree, they might have a contention.

"Only by pride cometh contention [conflict]" (Proverbs 13:10).

Corrupt: behaving in a dishonest or immoral way, often for selfish reasons or to take advantage of others. For example, if someone cheats on a test to get a better grade, they are being corrupt.

"But a corrupt [dishonest] tree bringeth forth evil fruit" (Matthew 7:17).

Council: a meeting of a group of people to talk about and decide on important issues. A town council may be a meeting of elected officials who meet to make decisions about local issues.

"Then the Pharisees went out, and held a council [meeting] against him" (Matthew 12:14).

Countenance: the look on a person's face that shows their mood or feelings. For example, if someone has a happy countenance, their face might have a smile and bright eyes.

"Wherefore the king said unto me, Why is thy countenance [look on your face] sad, seeing thou art not sick?" (Nehemiah 2:2).

Covenant: an agreement or promise between a person and God. Getting baptized is a covenant a person makes to demonstrate their commitment to follow Jesus Christ.

"And I will remember my covenant [promise], which is between me and you and every living creature of all flesh" (Genesis 9:15).

Covet: to desire or want something another person has and feeling jealous or envious of them for having it. When you see your friend's new toy and wish you had it too, that could be considered coveting.

Daniel in the lion's den.

"Thou shalt not covet [envy] thy neighbour's house, thou shalt not covet [envy] thy neighbour's wife, nor his manservant, nor his maidservant, nor his ox, nor his ass, nor any thing that is thy neighbour's" (Exodus 20:17).

Crucify: Roman torture or execution method where a person is tied or nailed to a cross and raised upright to cause both pain and shame. In the Bible, Jesus was crucified, but was resurrected three days later.

"But they cried out, Away with him, away with him, crucify [execute] him. Pilate saith unto them, Shall I crucify [execute] your King?" (John 19:15).

Cubit: a linear measurement, usually the distance from a man's elbow to the tip of the longest finger. The average length of a cubit is about 17.5 inches or 44.5 cm.

"And he made a porch of pillars; the length thereof was fifty cubits [24.3 yards], and the breadth thereof thirty cubits [14.6 yards]" (1 Kings 7:6).

Cumbered: to feel burdened or distracted by something to the point of feeling like it is hard to go on. For example, if you are carrying a heavy backpack and find it difficult to walk or run, you could say that you are cumbered by the weight of the backpack.

"But Martha was cumbered [burdened] about much serving" (Luke 10:40).

Damned: to be doomed or condemned to hell because of bad behavior or unwillingness to believe the truth. For instance, a mass murderer might be someone who would be damned.

"He that believeth not shall be damned [doomed]" (Mark 16:16).

Darken: to go dim or to grow less light or clear. Darken is the opposite of brighten. For example, if you close the curtains in a room, the room may darken because less light is coming in.

"I will cause the sun to go down at noon, and I will darken [dim] the earth in the clear day" (Amos 8:9).

Darkness: to lack light or truth for physical or spiritual sight. Darkness can occur during the nighttime when the sun has set, or when someone doesn't know the truth about something.

"As the blind gropeth in darkness [lack of light], and thou shalt not prosper in thy ways" (Deuteronomy 28:29).

Deaf: a person who is unable to hear or has a significant hearing loss. When someone is deaf, they are unable to perceive sound through their ears.

"Thou shalt not curse the deaf [people who can't hear], nor put a stumblingblock before the blind" (Leviticus 19:14).

Dearth: a scarcity or shortage of something, especially a shortage of food, resources, or supplies. For example, if there is a dearth of rain in an area, it means that there is not enough rainwater to help crops grow.

"And the seven years of dearth [scarcity] began to come, according as Joseph had said" (Genesis 41:54).

Deceit: the act of being dishonest or misleading in order to trick or deceive someone. It involves deliberately lying or distorting the truth with the intention of misleading others.

"Take heed that no man deceive [misleads] you" (Matthew 24:4).

Declare: to state, teach, or announce something clearly, openly, and formally. When you declare your love for someone, you openly express your feelings for them.

"I the Lord speak righteousness, I declare [openly state] things that are right" (Isaiah 45:19).

Decree: an order or command given by an authority figure. For example, a king might issue a decree to command his subjects to do something.

"He hath made a decree [an order] which shall not pass" (Psalm 148:6).

Dedication: the setting apart or devoting something for special use, particularly for the Lord. In the Bible, a dedication of Solomon's Temple was held to make it holy and devote it to God.

"And at the dedication [setting apart] of the wall of Jerusalem they sought the Levites out of all their places, to bring them to Jerusalem" (Nehemiah 12:27).

Defile: to make unclean, dirty, or impure; to corrupt. For example, if you write graffiti on a clean wall, you would defile the surface.

"Therefore he requested of the prince of the eunuchs that he might not defile himself [make himself unclean]" (Daniel 1:8).

Delight: to have or take great pleasure in something. For instance, eating an ice cream cone on a hot day can bring delight to a person.

"He retaineth not his anger for ever, because he delighteth [takes pleasure] in mercy" (Micah 7:18).

Deliver: to rescue, save, liberate, or set someone free from being held prisoner or captive. When a police officer rescues a hostage, they have been delivered to safety.

"I am come down to deliver [rescue] them out of the hand of the Egyptians" (Exodus 3:8).

Deny: to express a negative response, or to refuse to accept or allow something. When a child asks to eat a cookie before dinner and the parent says, "No," the parent is denying the child's request. Past tense: denied.

"And he confessed, and denied [refused] not" (John 1:20).

Descend: to come down from a higher place. When you walk down the stairs, hike down a mountain, or take an elevator to a lower floor, you are descending.

"For the Lord himself shall descend [come down] from heaven with a shout" (1 Thessalonians 4:16).

Desolate: a place or situation that is ruined, bleak, or abandoned. For example, a desert landscape with no vegetation or human habitation can be described as desolate.

"Your country is desolate [ruined], your cities are burned with fire" (Isaiah 1:7).

Despair: a feeling of utter hopelessness, sadness, or loss of faith or confidence. For example, someone who has failed a test may feel despair about their grade in the class.

"We are perplexed, but not in despair [utter hopelessness]" (2 Corinthians 4:8).

Devil: a lesser evil spirit causing trouble for humans. In the Bible it is sometimes used as another name for Satan or a follower of Satan.

"Many will say to me in that day, Lord, Lord, have we not prophesied in thy name? and in thy name have cast out devils [lesser evil spirits]?" (Matthew 7:22).

Diligent: to give constant effort to accomplish a goal or task. A person who keeps trying, even after failing multiple times, might be described as diligent.

"But take diligent [give constant effort] heed to do the commandment and the law" (Joshua 22:5).

Disciple: a person who follows and obeys Christ. In the New Testament, disciple is also used to refer to the 12 apostles Jesus chose during His ministry.

"Then said Jesus to those Jews which believed on him, If ye continue in my word, then are ye my disciples [followers] indeed" (John 8:31).

Dispensation: a religious period of time in which God interacts with humanity in a specific way, revealing His plan and expectations for people during that time. For example, the time that Adam and Eve spent in the Garden of Eden was one dispensation, and the time after the Fall began a new dispensation.

"That in the dispensation [time period] of the fulness of times he might gather together in one all things in Christ" (Ephesians 1:10).

Disperse: to scatter or separate and send off or drive in different directions. A group of people may disperse after a meeting, moving in different directions to go home.

"And he shall set up an ensign for the nations, and shall assemble the outcasts of Israel, and gather together the dispersed [scattered] of Judah" (Isaiah 11:12).

Dispute: to argue about something or to discuss a point. When two countries argue over a border issue, it is called a dispute.

"Yet Michael the archangel, when contending with the devil he disputed [argued] about the body of Moses" (Jude 1:9).

Divers: an old-fashioned term that typically means several, various, or a variety of something. For example, "There were divers toys in the box" would mean "There were a variety of toys in the box."

"My brethren, count it all joy when ye fall into divers [a variety of] temptations" (James 1:2).

Doctrine: a set of religious values or principles held as true. One doctrine or truth of Christianity taught in the Bible is that Jesus is the Son of God.

"My doctrine [values] shall drop as the rain" (Deuteronomy 32:2).

Dominion: to have power of control or authority over something. For example, a queen may have dominion over a kingdom.

"Death hath no more dominion [power] over him" (Romans 6:9).

Doubt: a feeling of uncertainty or not being sure about the truth, accuracy, or reliability of something. For example, a student may have doubt about the correctness of an answer on a test.

"How long dost thou make us to doubt [uncertain]? If thou be the Christ, tell us plainly" (John 10:24).

Draw: to bring, pull, or carry something. For instance, when you wind up the string of a flying kite, you will draw the kit down from the sky. Past tense: drew.

"Draw [bring] nigh to God, and he will draw [bring] nigh to you" (James 4:8).

Dread: a strong feeling of fear, apprehension, or anticipation of something unpleasant or threatening. When a person goes to the dentist, they may have a feeling of dread.

"Dread [fear] not, neither be afraid of them" (Deuteronomy 1:29).

Dross: any worthless or inferior material that is separated or discarded from a valuable or desirable substance. When gold or silver is refined, the impurities that are removed are called dross.

"Son of man, the house of Israel is to me become dross [impure]" (Ezekiel 22:18).

Drought: a continuous lack of rain, which often leads to famine. When a drought occurs, farmers have a hard time watering their crops and getting the plants to grow.

"And I called for a drought [lack of rain] upon the land, and upon the mountains" (Haggai 1:11).

Drunkard: a person who tends to drink too much alcohol or gets drunk frequently. In the Bible, being a drunkard is described as unhealthy and bad.

"Awake, ye drunkards [people who drink too much], and weep" (Joel 1:5).

Due Time: occurs or is finished at the right or expected time. For example, if a project is due on Friday, completing it by Friday would be considered doing it in due time.

"Who gave himself a ransom for all, to be testified in due time [at the right time]" (1 Timothy 2:6).

Dung: to fertilize plants with manure. Dung is created from the excrement of animals and contains nutrients that can be beneficial for plant growth.

"Lord, let it alone this year also, till I shall dig about it, and dung [fertilize] it" (Luke 13:8).

Durst: an old word that means to dare or to try to do something risky. "He durst not speak up in class for fear of getting in trouble" means "He did not dare to speak up in class for fear of getting in trouble."

"And no man was able to answer him a word, neither durst [dared] any man from that day forth ask him any more questions" (Matthew 22:46).

Duty: a responsibility or obligation that someone has to do or fulfill. For example, a citizen has a duty to follow laws and contribute to society.

"Fear God, and keep his commandments: for this is the whole duty [responsibility] of man" (Ecclesiastes 12:13).

Dwell: to live in or reside somewhere. A person might dwell in an apartment, a house, or even a tent.

"I will dwell [live] in the house of the Lord for ever" (Psalm 23:6).

Earnest: an adjective describing someone who is sincere, serious, and committed to a particular course of action or belief. A person who is earnest about helping the poor might donate money to or volunteer at a shelter.

"Therefore we ought to give the more earnest [sincere] heed to the things which we have heard" (Hebrews 2:1).

Ease: a person who is at rest, at peace, or in comfort. When school gets out for the summer, students are more at ease because they do not have homework to do.

"And I am very sore displeased with the heathen that are at ease [rest]" (Zechariah 1:15).

Eden: the garden where Adam and Eve lived before the Fall. While living in the Garden of Eden, Adam and Eve were tempted to eat the fruit of the Tree of Life.

"And he will make her wilderness like Eden [a garden]" (Isaiah 51:3).

Edify: to instruct or enlighten someone in a way that promotes learning, moral or intellectual development, or spiritual growth. For example, a teacher may seek to edify their students by providing clear explanations, examples, and guidance.

"Wherefore comfort yourselves together, and edify [instruct] one another" (1 Thessalonians 5:11).

Elder: religious leaders who hold an office in the Melchizedek priesthood. According to the New Testament, an elder is responsible for leading in the church, teaching and preaching, visiting the sick, and protecting the saints.

"And the saying pleased Absalom well, and all the elders [religious leaders] of Israel" (2 Samuel 17:4).

Elect: righteous people who are called of God to be in His service. Moses, Noah, and Abraham were all elect men who were called as prophets because of their righteousness.

"And mine elect [righteous people] shall inherit it" (Isaiah 65:9).

Embrace: a hug; to wrap your arms around something or someone with affection or enthusiasm. A teddy bear may be embraced tightly for comfort.

"A time to embrace [hug], and a time to refrain from embracing [hugging]" (Ecclesiastes 3:5).

Endure: to last a long time; to persist or withstand something difficult, challenging, or unpleasant without giving up or giving in. For example, a person may endure physical pain during an illness or injury.

"The glory of the Lord shall endure [last a long time] for ever" (Psalm 104:31).

Enlarge: to grow, widen, or increase in size. When a family adds a new room to their house, it is enlarged.

"Enlarge [grow] the place of thy tent" (Isaiah 54:2).

Enlighten: to brighten or add light to a space. Symbolically, enlighten also means to give someone information so they become more informed or knowledgeable. When a teacher explains a complex topic in simple terms, the students might be enlightened.

"The Lord my God will enlighten [brighten] my darkness" (Psalm 18:28).

Enmity: a deep-seated dislike or hostility towards a person, group, idea, or concept. For example, two people who are constantly arguing and showing dislike towards each other may be said to have enmity between them.

"Or in enmity [with feelings of hostility] smite him with his hand, that he die" (Numbers 35:21).

Ensign: a distinctive flag or banner that is used to identify or represent a particular group, such as a military unit, a naval vessel, or a country. On British naval ships, the Red Ensign is typically flown to identify its nationality.

"Every man of the children of Israel shall pitch by his own standard, with the ensign [flag] of their father's house" (Numbers 2:2).

Entreat: to earnestly ask or beg someone for something, often in a polite or pleading manner. For example, if you ask your friend to lend you a pencil because you forgot yours, you might say, "Please, can you entreat me with a pencil? I really need one for class."

"Entreat [ask] me not to leave thee, or to return from following after thee" (Ruth 1:16).

Envy: to be jealous of or to have ill will toward someone. When you see a friend riding a new bike that you have been wanting, you might get feelings of envy.

"For he knew that for envy [jealousy] they had delivered him" (Matthew 27:18).

Ephah: a volume measure used for dry substances, like flour. Typically, an ephah measured about eight gallons.

"Now an omer is the tenth part of an ephah [eight gallons]" (Exodus 16:36).

Epistle: a letter meant to be read to a group of people or congregation. If your bishop or pastor was out of town, but wanted to send a message to the congregation, they might write an epistle to be read over the pulpit.

"I charge you by the Lord that this epistle [letter] be read unto all the holy brethren" (1 Thessalonians 5:27).

Equity: everyone is treated in a fair and impartial manner, without favoritism or discrimination. If a parent gives their children the same amount of allowance each week, it would be a way of promoting equity.

"He walked with me in peace and equity [impartiality]" (Malachi 2:6).

Err: to go astray, make a mistake, or to make an error. For example, if you accidentally add 2 + 2 and get 5, you would have erred in your calculation.

"Jesus answered and said unto them, Ye do err [mistake], not knowing the scriptures, nor the power of God" (Matthew 22:29).

Espouse: to marry or the state of being married. In the Old Testament, Abraham and Sarah were espoused.

"When as his mother Mary was espoused [married] to Joseph" (Matthew 1:18).

Establish: to set up, create, or start something, typically with the intention of making it permanent or official. When you start a lemonade stand in your front yard with a table, some cups, and a sign, you would be establishing a business.

"Thy seed will I establish [set up] for ever" (Psalm 89:4).

Estate: a time frame of being or existence. In the Bible, the first estate typically refers to premortal life, while the second estate indicates mortal life on earth.

"And the angels which kept not their first estate [premortal life], but left their own habitation" (Jude 1:6).

Elijah and the ravens.

Eternal: something that lasts forever or goes on indefinitely, without an end. Traditionally, God is described as an eternal being who has lived forever.

"And being made perfect, he became the author of eternal [endless] salvation" (Hebrews 5:9).

Everlasting: to endure forever. Everlasting is a synonym for the word "eternal." For example, if you have a toy that never breaks or wears out, you might describe it as everlasting.

"His dominion is an everlasting [eternal] dominion, which shall not pass away" (Daniel 7:14).

Evil: something that is morally wrong, wicked, or harmful. For instance, stealing, hurting others intentionally, or lying to deceive someone are considered evil acts.

"Yea, though I walk through the valley of the shadow of death, I will fear no evil [wickedness]" (Psalm 23:4).

Exalt: to raise up to heaven, to glorify, or to praise. In the Bible, when Jesus is resurrected and raised up to heaven, He was exalted.

"Exalt [raise up to heaven] him that is low, and abase him that is high" (Ezekiel 21:26).

Exhort: to strongly urge, advise, or encourage someone to do something. For example, if you strongly encourage your friend to study hard for an upcoming test, you are exhorting them to put in effort and do their best.

"Holding fast the faithful word as he hath been taught, that he may be able by sound doctrine both to exhort [encourage] and to convince the gainsayers" (Titus 1:9).

Expedient: something that is practical, convenient, or advantageous for achieving a specific goal or purpose. When you choose to take a shortcut to get to school quickly, even though it might not be the safest route, it could be considered expedient.

"All things are lawful unto me, but all things are not expedient [practical]" (1 Corinthians 6:12).

Faint: a word that describes when something is very weak or not clear. For example, if a person ran a long distance, they might feel faint afterwards.

"Men ought always to pray, and not to faint [be weak]" (Luke 18:1).

Faith: trusting in something even when you don't have all the answers or when there may be doubts or uncertainties. It's like having confidence or trust in something or someone even when you can't explain or prove it logically.

"And the apostles said unto the Lord, Increase our faith [trust]" (Luke 17:5)

Fall: to stumble, lose your balance, or to fail. When you trip over a toy, you might fall to the ground. In the Bible, Adam and Eve's eating the fruit of the Tree of Life, and their dismissal from Eden, is known as the Fall.

"He that diggeth a pit shall fall [stumble] into it" (Ecclesiastes 10:8).

False: something that is not true or accurate. It means that it is not based on facts or reality, and it can be the opposite of "true." If a person said the world is flat, their comment would be considered false.

"Yea, and we are found false [not true] witnesses of God" (1 Corinthians 15:15).

Famine: period of widespread hunger that leads to suffering or starvation. In the Old Testament, Joseph of Egypt helped prepare the people to go through a seven-year famine by storing up food in advance.

"And there was a great famine [period of hunger] in Samaria" (2 Kings 6:25).

Farthing: an old-fashioned British word for one-fourth of a penny. Farthings were made of copper and were typically small and round coins, with a design or a portrait of a monarch on one side and a number on the other side.

"Are not two sparrows sold for a farthing [small amount of money]?" (Matthew 10:29).

Fashion: the way people behave or do things in a particular time period or culture. The traditions and customs of a people help to shape the fashion or appearance of their culture.

"For the fashion [traditions] of this world passeth away" (1 Corinthians 7:31).

Fast: the Bible uses the word fast in two different ways.
Definition 1: to grip tightly or firmly onto something and not let go. If you are climbing a tree, you might have to hold fast to a branch to make sure you don't fall.

"Hold that fast [firmly] which thou hast, that no man take thy crown" (Revelation 3:11).

Definition 2: the practice of voluntarily abstaining from food or drink for a certain period of time in an effort to draw closer to God. In some churches, fasting once a month is a regular practice.

"Fast [don't eat food] ye for me, and neither eat nor drink three days, night or day" (Esther 4:16).

Fault: a word that describes when something is wrong or not working properly because of a deficiency, flaw, or shortcoming. For example, if a car's engine stops running, there may be a "fault" in the engine, meaning there is something wrong with it that needs to be fixed.

"I find no fault [shortcoming] in this man" (Luke 23:4).

Favour: an act of kindness or a special preference shown to someone, usually through approval, praise, or esteem. If your teacher has a favorite student, they may show them "favour" by giving them extra attention or privileges.

"A good man sheweth favour [kindness], and lendeth" (Psalm 112:5).

Fear: the feeling of being worried or afraid, often in response to a perceived threat or danger. In the Bible, sometimes the word "fear" is also used to mean reverence for God. When Saul was confronted by an angel on the road to Damascus, he began to fear God and be obedient.

"Fear [worry] and dread shall fall upon them" (Exodus 15:16).

Feeble: something that is weak, frail, or lacking in strength or vigor. After a person has surgery, they might feel feeble and weak during their recovery.

"Strengthen ye the weak hands, and confirm the feeble [weak] knees" (Isaiah 35:3).

Feebleminded: something that is mentally weak or frail. For instance, when a person cries easily or worries all the time, they might be described as feebleminded.

"Comfort the feebleminded [mentally weak], support the weak, be patient toward all men" (1 Thessalonians 5:14).

Fellowship: friendly association or companionship among people who share similar interests, beliefs, or activities. When a group of people who share the same religious beliefs gather to worship, they may refer to it as a fellowship.

"That which we have seen and heard declare we unto you, that ye also may have fellowship [association] with us" (1 John 1:3).

Fervent: having a deeply sincere belief in something. For example, if someone is very enthusiastic and passionate about protecting the environment, they may be described as having a "fervent" commitment to it.

"The effectual fervent [deeply sincere] prayer of a righteous man availeth much" (James 5:16).

Fiery: a word that means flaming or blazing like a fire. A dragon's breath might be described as fiery.

"Thou shalt make them as a fiery [flaming] oven in the time of thine anger" (Psalm 21:9).

Fig: a type of fruit from the fig tree, which grows in warm climates. Figs are sweet and used to make cookies, cakes, and other baked goods.

"Do men gather grapes of thorns, or figs [type of fruit] of thistles?" (Matthew 7:16).

Filth: material that is considered offensive or morally objectionable. If someone uses vulgar language or tells inappropriate jokes, their speech may be described as "filth."

"We are made as the filth [morally offensive] of the world" (1 Corinthians 4:13).

Firmament: the expanse of the sky or heavens, especially as seen from the Earth. In ancient times it was believed that the firmament was a dome-like structure that separated the Earth from the heavens.

"And they that be wise shall shine as the brightness of the firmament [sky]" (Daniel 12:3).

Firstfruit: the earliest portion of a harvest or flock produced, which is seen as being owned by the Lord. In the Old Testament, Able gave the firstfruits of his flocks (first born lambs) to the Lord.

"Honour the Lord with thy substance, and with the firstfruits [first portion of harvest] of all thine increase" (Proverbs 3:9).

Firstling: the first baby animals born or plants grown in spring. For example, if a cow gives birth to its first calf, that calf may be referred to as the "firstling" of the cow.

"And Abel, he also brought of the firstlings [first baby animals] of his flock and of the fat thereof" (Genesis 4:4).

Fitly: an adverb that describes the manner in which something is done or performed, indicating that it is done in a suitable, appropriate, or proper manner. If someone completes their math homework correctly, it might be described as being done "fitly."

"In whom all the building fitly [properly] framed together groweth unto an holy temple in the Lord" (Ephesians 2:21).

Fixed: physically unmovable or unchangeable in position. Fixed may also be used to describe something that is determined, unwavering, or resolute. When a person has a firm opinion or decision about something, their stance may be referred to as "fixed."

"His heart is fixed [determined], trusting in the Lord" (Psalm 112:7).

Flatter: the act of giving undeserved praise or to sweet-talk someone. When a person wants you to do them a favor, they might first flatter you with a few compliments.

"Their throat is an open sepulchre; they flatter [give undeserved praise] with their tongue" (Psalm 5:9).

Flee: to run away from or escape from danger or a threat. If you came across a snake while out hiking, you might flee away from it to avoid harm.

"As if a man did flee [run away] from a lion, and a bear met him" (Amos 5:19).

Flesh and Blood: a biblical term for mortality or human existence. In the Bible we learn that although humans have bodies of flesh and blood that will die, God is immortal and will not die.

"For we wrestle not against flesh and blood [mortality], but against principalities" (Ephesians 6:12).

Flock: literally, a flock is a herd or group of animals that stay together. For example, a group of birds, such as ducks or geese, flying or feeding together is called a "flock" of birds. Symbolically, a flock is a church congregation or group of believers.

"Now Moses kept the flock [herd] of Jethro his father in law" (Exodus 3:1).

Foes: enemies, people, or things that are opposed or hostile to each other. For instance, in a game or competition, teams or players that are competing against each other may be considered as "foes."

"Until I make thy foes [enemies] thy footstool" (Acts 2:35).

Fold: a pen or enclosure for a herd of sheep or other farm animals. A shepherd will keep his sheep in a fold at night, where they would be safe and protected from predators.

"And other sheep I have, which are not of this fold [enclosure]" (John 10:16).

Folly: when someone displays foolish behavior or a lack of good judgment. For example, if someone makes a poor decision or behaves in a silly or thoughtless way, it could be described as "folly."

"The instruction of fools is folly [foolish]" (Proverbs 16:22).

Forbear: to refrain from doing something, to patiently tolerate or endure, or to hold back from reacting or responding to a situation. When someone resists the urge to interrupt others while they are speaking, they are said to "forbear" from interrupting.

"Yet many years didst thou forbear [tolerate] them" (Nehemiah 9:30).

Forbid: to command someone not to do something, or to refuse to give someone permission to do something. When a parent tells their child not to eat candy before dinner, they are "forbidding" the child from doing so. Past tense: forbade.

"Can any man forbid [refuse] water, that these should not be baptized …" (Acts 10:47).

Foreordained: given an assignment or plan before being born into the world. In the Bible, John the Baptist was foreordained with the assignment to baptize and testify of Jesus Christ as the Son of God.

"But with the precious blood of Christ, as of a lamb without blemish and without spot: Who verily was foreordained [given an assignment] before the foundation of the world" (1 Peter 1:19–20).

Forgive: the action of pardoning a fault, error, or sin without holding it against them or seeking revenge. If someone says something hurtful to you and later expresses genuine remorse, you might choose to forgive them and let it go.

"He will not forgive [pardon] your transgressions nor your sins" (Joshua 24:19).

Forsake: to leave or abandon someone or something permanently. For example, if someone decides to leave a toy they used to play with outside and never go back to retrieve it, they are "forsaking" the toy. Past tense: forsook.

"If ye seek him, he will be found of you; but if ye forsake [abandon] him, he will forsake [leave] you" (2 Chronicles 15:2).

Frankincense: an incense made from tree gum resin and used for priesthood ordinances in ancient times. When frankincense is burned it produces an aromatic smell. It is extremely valuable because of its rarity and its ability to heal.

"And cinnamon, and odours, and ointments, and frankincense [incense]" (Revelation 18:13).

Freely: to treat generously or to give readily, without holding anything back. For example, if someone is allowed to choose their own favorite color without any influence from others, they are choosing "freely."

"When they came to the house of the Lord which is at Jerusalem, offered freely [generously] for the house of God" (Ezra 2:68).

Fruitful: a biblical term meaning to have children, or to live in such a way as to produce the "fruit of the spirit" (Galatians 5:22-23). Adam and Eve were commanded by God to be fruitful when they were placed in the Garden of Eden.

"God blessed them, saying, Be fruitful [have children]" (Genesis 1:22).

Fulness: to live in a manner that yields abundance or plenty. For example, someone who is brimming with happiness can be described as having a "fulness" of joy.

"That ye might be filled with all the fulness [abundance] of God" (Ephesians 3:19).

Fury: a state of anger or rage. If someone was to burn your house down and cause injury to your family, you might feel a sense of fury.

"I beseech thee, let thine anger and thy fury [anger] be turned away from thy city Jerusalem" (Daniel 9:16).

Gainsaying: the act of contradicting or disputing something. For example, if someone says, "The sky is blue," and another person responds with "No, it's not, it's gray," that would be an example of gainsaying.

"But to Israel he saith, All day long I have stretched forth my hands unto a disobedient and gainsaying [contradicting] people" (Romans 10:21).

Garment: a piece of clothing or apparel. A T-shirt is a type of garment that people wear on their upper body, while jeans are a type of garment worn on the legs.

"Lo, they all shall wax old as a garment [piece of clothing]; the moth shall eat them up" (Isaiah 50:9).

Gentile: a person not of the House of Israel or of the Jewish faith. Gentile is a synonym for heathen or pagan. Although gentile can have a negative quality to it, in Hebrew it simply means "the nations."

"Then hath God also to the Gentiles [non-Jewish people] granted repentance unto life" (Acts 11:18).

Gird: to bind, fasten, or secure something tightly around oneself or an object, usually with a belt, band, or strap. For example, if someone puts on a belt to hold up their pants, they are girding their waist with the belt.

"For this gird [bind] you with sackcloth" (Jeremiah 4:8).

Girdle: a belt or sash worn around the waist. In Biblical times, a girdle was worn for ceremonial or symbolic purposes, such as a sash worn by a high priest serving in the temple.

"And when he was come unto us, he took Paul's girdle [belt], and bound his own hands and feet" (Acts 21:11).

Glean: to gather together, especially grain left by the reapers of a harvest. In the Old Testament, Ruth worked to glean grain from the fields to use as food for Naomi and herself.

"Thus saith the Lord of hosts, They shall throughly glean [gather together] the remnant of Israel as a vine" (Jeremiah 6:9).

Glorify: to give praise or honor to someone in a way that makes them seem more important. For example, if someone receives an award for their achievements and others praise and honor them for their accomplishments, they are being glorified.

"I will be sanctified in them that come nigh me, and before all the people I will be glorified [praised]" (Leviticus 10:3).

Glorious: to be splendid, magnificent, or awe-inspiring in appearance. For instance, a beautiful rainbow after a rainstorm can be described as glorious.

"Strengthened with all might, according to his glorious [splendid] power" (Colossians 1:11).

Glory: great honor, praise, or admiration that is given to someone or something. When someone wins a gold medal in the Olympics, they receive glory for their outstanding performance.

"For thine is the kingdom, and the power, and the glory [honor], for ever" (Matthew 6:13).

Gnash: to grind one's the teeth together when angry. A dog might gnash its teeth of a stranger approaches it's territory.

"All thine enemies have opened their mouth against thee: they hiss and gnash [grind] the teeth" (Lamentations 2:16).

Goad: the act of poking, pricking, or provoking, particularly a work animal. The word goad comes from the name of a tool, sometimes called a gad, used to poke oxen pulling a plow to get them to move.

"The words of the wise are as goads [pricks], and as nails fastened by the masters of assemblies, which are given from one shepherd" (Ecclesiastes 12:11).

The Good Shepherd

Godliness: careful obedience and faithfulness the commandments of God; devout or righteous. Someone who consistently displays kindness, compassion, and honesty in their actions might be described as godly.

"Godliness [righteousness] is profitable unto all things" (1 Timothy 4:8).

Goodly: something that is admirable, attractive, or outstanding. Many prophets or prophetesses in the Bible are generally considered to be goodly people.

"And Joseph was a goodly [admirable] person, and well favoured" (Genesis 39:6).

Gospel: in Greek the word gospel literally means "good news." In the Bible, Jesus Christ's gospel is His doctrine or His teachings and Atonement, namely faith, repentance, baptism, and the gift of the Holy Ghost.

"And he said unto them, Go ye into all the world, and preach the gospel [Christ's doctrine] to every creature" (Mark 16:15).

Grace: the unconditional love, forgiveness, and favor that God shows towards people, even when they don't deserve it. It's like a special gift or blessing that God gives to everyone, regardless of their mistakes or shortcomings. Grace is made possible by the Atonement of Jesus Christ.

"But we believe that through the grace [forgiveness] of the Lord Jesus Christ we shall be saved, even as they" (Acts 15:11).

Gracious: the act of being loving or being filled with God's love. Treating people with kindness, even when they are mean to you, would be considered gracious.

"And all bare him witness, and wondered at the gracious [loving] words which proceeded out of his mouth" (Luke 4:22).

Graven: cutting or carving into something hard, like wood or stone, to create a design or picture. Some artists make sculptures through a process that could be described as graven.

"Thy graven [carved] images also will I cut off, and thy standing images out of the midst of thee" (Micah 5:13).

Greedy: the desire to have more than your fair share or an unwillingness to share; covetous. When a toddler takes all the cookies and won't share, she might be described as greedy.

"He that is greedy [wants more than his fair share] of gain troubleth his own house" (Proverbs 15:27).

Grief: the feeling of deep sorrow or heartache; misery. When someone experiences a death in the family, they often feel grief and sadness.

"For in much wisdom is much grief [sorrow]" (Ecclesiastes 1:18).

Grieve: to mourn or be distressed over someone who has died or something that is lost. It's like feeling very, very sad and missing someone or something that is no longer with us. Past tense: grieved.

"I Daniel was grieved [distressed] in my spirit in the midst of my body" (Daniel 7:15).

Grievous: something that is hard or heavy to bear; something serious. For example, a grievous injury could be a very serious or severe injury that causes a lot of pain or discomfort.

"And his commandments are not grievous [hard to bear]" (1 John 5:3).

Guile: dishonesty, cleverness, or slyness in a tricky or deceitful way. It's like being sneaky or cunning in order to achieve a goal or get what you want.

"Wherefore laying aside all malice, and all guile [dishonesty], and hypocrisies" (1 Peter 2:1).

Habitation: a home or house for people or animals. Habitation can refer to different types of places, such as houses, apartments, caves, nests, or dens, where living creatures find shelter and make their homes.

"Look down from thy holy habitation [home], from heaven, and bless thy people Israel" (Deuteronomy 26:15).

Hallow: to make something holy or to set apart. For example, you might say that a church or a cemetery is hallowed ground, meaning it is considered sacred or holy.

"Hallow [make holy] ye the sabbath day, as I commanded your fathers" (Jeremiah 17:22).

Halt: to stop or to come to a sudden pause of movement. When a car comes to a sudden stop at a red light it might be described as coming to a halt.

"How long halt [stop] ye between two opinions?" (1 Kings 18:21).

Handmaid: an old-fashioned term meaning a female servant to a mistress. In the Bible, Hagar was a handmaid to Sarah, wife of Abraham.

"Behold the handmaid [female servant] of the Lord" (Luke 1:38).

Hardened or Hardness: something that has become physically or emotionally tough, rigid, or resistant to change. For example, after a person goes through many trials, they might become more hardened from their life experiences.

"He hath blinded their eyes, and hardened [made rigid] their heart" (John 12:40).

Harlot: an adulteress or prostitute; a woman who disobeys the law of chastity. In the Bible harlots were banned from society and considered outcasts.

"How is the faithful city become an harlot [adulteress]!" (Isaiah 1:21).

Harrow: to torment or cause suffering for someone or something. For example, someone might say, "The tragic news harrowed his heart."

"Will he harrow [torment] the valleys after thee?" (Job 39:10).

Hasten: to hurry, or to speed up a process, or to do something with urgency. For instance, warm spring weather might hasten the melting of snow on the mountains.

"For I will hasten [hurry] my word to perform it" (Jeremiah 1:12).

Haughty: to be proud, stuck-up, or arrogant, often looking down upon others. A person might say, "His haughty behavior made it difficult for others to approach him."

"An haughty [proud] spirit before a fall" (Proverbs 16:18).

Hearken: to readily listen to, or to attend to with the intent of obeying. When a student hearkens to a teacher's instructions, they are likely to do well on the assignment.

"How shall Pharaoh hearken [listen] unto me?" (Exodus 6:30).

Heathen: a gentile; someone who does not acknowledge God as described in the Bible. Although heathen can have a negative quality to it, in Hebrew it simply means "the nations."

"And all such as had separated themselves unto them from the filthiness of the heathen [gentiles] of the land" (Ezra 6:21).

Heavenly: something that is divine, celestial, or beautiful, like heaven would be. A beautiful garden might be described as heavenly.

"Wherefore, holy brethren, partakers of the heavenly [divine] calling" (Hebrews 3:1).

Hebrew: someone who belongs to the Hebrew ethnic group or identifies with the Hebrew culture and language. Hebrew people are generally associated with the Jewish faith. In the Bible, the Hebrew people are called Jews or Israel.

"He spied an Egyptian smiting an Hebrew [Jew], one of his brethren" (Exodus 2:11).

Hedge: to surround something with a wall or fence, sometimes made of bushes or plants. Figuratively, "hedge up" can mean to create obstacles or difficulties in order to prevent or limit something from happening.

"Therefore, behold, I will hedge up [create obstacles in] thy way with thorns" (Hosea 2:6).

Heed: to pay careful attention to something, take notice of it, and act accordingly. If a parent asks a child to heed their instructions, they are asking them to listen carefully and be obedient.

"Take heed [pay careful attention] to the ministry which thou hast received in the Lord, that thou fulfil it" (Colossians 4:17).

Heir: a person who is a successor; someone who receives an inheritance or birthright. A prince or princess would be an heir to a King and would be expected to eventually sit on the throne.

"We should be made heirs [successor] according to the hope of eternal life" (Titus 3:7).

Henceforth: an old-fashioned word meaning "from this time forward." If a teacher says, "Henceforth, all assignments must be submitted online," it means that starting from now, all assignments must be submitted electronically.

"When thou tillest the ground, it shall not henceforth [from this time forward] yield unto thee her strength" (Genesis 4:12).

Herald: an officer in the military whose job was to make deliver announcements or make proclamations of war, peace, etc. Historically, a herald often traveled on horseback or foot to convey messages between different units or locations on the battlefield or during times of war.

"Then an herald [officer] cried aloud, To you it is commanded" (Daniel 3:4).

Heresy: teachings that go against God's commandments or doctrine. Sometimes heresy is called false doctrine. For example, if someone taught that lying, stealing, or cheating were okay, that would be considered heresy or false doctrine.

"But this I confess unto thee, that after the way which they call heresy [false doctrine], so worship I the God of my fathers" (Acts 24:14).

Heritage: cultural, historical, or natural legacy that is passed down from previous generations and preserved for future generations. A heritage might include traditions, customs, beliefs, values, practices, and artifacts that are inherited and valued by a particular group.

"I will give it you for an heritage [legacy]: I am the Lord" (Exodus 6:8).

Hewn: to cut or shape something with force, typically using tools or equipment, in order to create a desired form or shape. For instance, if a carpenter uses a saw or an axe to cut down a tree and shape it into wooden planks, they are hewing the wood.

"And laid it in his own new tomb, which he had hewn [cut] out in the rock" (Matthew 27:60).

Highway: a large public road that connects towns and cities. In Jesus's day, Roman engineers learned how to make roads sturdy and built an interconnected road system throughout the entire Empire.

"Bartimæus, the son of Timæus, sat by the highway [road] side begging" (Mark 10:46).

Hinder: to make something more difficult for someone, possibly causing harm or injury. For example, if you place a large rock in the middle of a path, it will hinder someone from walking or running smoothly on it.

"But suffer all things, lest we should hinder [make more difficult] the gospel of Christ" (1 Corinthians 9:12).

Hire: payment for an employee who provides work or services; wages. For example, an artist commissioned to create a mural for a school would be paid on a work for hire basis.

"The ringstraked shall be thy hire [payment]" (Genesis 31:8).

Hiss: the sound of a snake. When a startled cat sees a snake slither across the grass, it might arch its back and let out a loud hiss.

"I will hiss [make the sound of a snake] for them, and gather them" (Zechariah 10:8).

Holy: something that is sacred, pure, or consecrated to God. For instance, a church or temple may be considered a holy place because it is dedicated to religious worship.

"For I am the Lord that bringeth you up out of the land of Egypt, to be your God: ye shall therefore be holy [sacred], for I am holy [sacred]" (Leviticus 11:45).

Holy Ghost or Spirit: third person of the trinity or Godhead whose role is to testify of Christ. In the New Testament, when Jesus was baptized, the Holy Ghost's presence was manifested by the sign of the dove.

"For there are three that bear record in heaven, the Father, the Word, and the Holy Ghost [Testifier]: and these three are one" (1 John 5:7).

Honestly: telling the truth, being truthful, and acting in a sincere and genuine manner. If you admit when you make a mistake or take responsibility for your actions, you are acting honestly.

"That ye may walk honestly [truthfully] toward them that are without" (1 Thessalonians 4:12).

Honourable: someone who acts in a way that is worthy of respect and seen as fair or upright. For example, a person who keeps their promises, tells the truth, and treats others with kindness can be described as honourable.

"His work is honourable [worthy of respect] and glorious" (Psalm 111:3).

Hope: to trust in or have confidence in something, such as in God or salvation. In the Bible, the apostle Paul taught that by having patience and studying the scriptures we can have greater hope.

"The Lord will be the hope [confidence] of his people, and the strength of the children of Israel" (Joel 3:16).

Hosanna: a Hebrew word that means "save us now, we pray." "Hosanna in the highest!" is a phrase that is often used in Christian hymns and songs.

"And the multitudes that went before, and that followed, cried, saying, Hosanna [Save us] to the Son of David: Blessed is he that cometh in the name of the Lord; Hosanna [Save us] in the highest" (Matthew 21:9).

Hospitality: the practice of being welcoming or friendly to guests and travelers. For example, when you have a friend over at your house, you might offer them a drink to be hospitable.

"But a lover of hospitality [being friendly to guests], a lover of good men" (Titus 1:8).

Humility: recognizing and accepting one's limitations and mistakes without feeling superior or boastful. A person with humility has a modest attitude about themself and a repentant heart.

"Serving the Lord with all humility [modesty] of mind, and with many tears, and temptations" (Acts 20:19).

Husbandman: a person who is a farmer. A husbandman is responsible for the cultivation, care, and maintenance of crops, animals, or other agricultural resources.

"The husbandman [farmer] waiteth for the precious fruit of the earth" (James 5:7).

Hypocrite: someone who pretends to be different than who they really are; a pretender. A person who criticizes someone for cheating on a test, but was then found to have cheated too, would be a hypocrite.

"Woe unto you, scribes and Pharisees, hypocrites [pretenders]! for ye are as graves which appear not, and the men that walk over them are not aware of them" (Luke 11:44).

Hyssop: a plant found in Palestine that is used in Jewish purification rites. In the Bible, a branch of hyssop was used to sprinkle blood as part of the Jewish Passover celebration, making it symbolic of Jesus Christ.

"Purge me with hyssop [plant used to help purify], and I shall be clean" (Psalm 51:7).

Idle: to not be busy or employed, or not getting things done. When a video game is paused, and no one is playing it, it could be described as idle.

"An idle [unemployed] soul shall suffer hunger" (Proverbs 19:15).

Idolatry: the worship of statues, false gods, and images; or, when someone gives too much importance to something or someone in their life. In Bible times, some people worshipped statues that were representative of various pagan gods, like Ishtar, a goddess of love.

"For rebellion is as the sin of witchcraft, and stubbornness is as iniquity and idolatry [worshiping false gods]" (1 Samuel 15:23).

Ignorance: when someone is lacking in wisdom or knowledge; unaware. It's like when you don't know the answer to a question because you haven't studied that topic yet or when you're not aware of certain facts or information.
"For so is the will of God, that with well doing ye may put to silence the ignorance [lack of wisdom] of foolish men" (1 Peter 2:15).

Immortal: never dying, deathless, or endless. It is the opposite of mortal. Immortal is like when a character in a fairy tale or a superhero in a comic book doesn't age or can't be killed.

"Now unto the King eternal, immortal [never dying], invisible, the only wise God" (1 Timothy 1:17).

Incense: an offering of perfume or nice fragrance. Incense is often used during religious or spiritual ceremonies, or to create a calming or relaxing atmosphere in a room.

"Let my prayer be set forth before thee as incense [offering of perfume]" (Psalm 141:2).

Incorruption: something that is free from mortal decline caused by age or disease. For example, when food never goes bad or spoils it might be described as incorruptible.

"It is sown in corruption; it is raised in incorruption [free from mortal decline]" (1 Corinthians 15:42).

Increase: growth in size or number, such as of worldly goods, money, or children. In Hebrew, the same word for "multiply" (as in "multiply and replenish the earth") is used for increase.

"And the tree of the field shall yield her fruit, and the earth shall yield her increase [growth]" (Ezekiel 34:27).

Indignation: to be angry or displeased at something that seems unjust or unfair. It's like when you feel really upset because you or someone else has been treated unfairly, or when you see something happening that you believe is wrong.

"But when his disciples saw it, they had indignation [anger]" (Matthew 26:8).

Infirmities: illnesses, sicknesses, or diseases that people suffer from. For example, when someone has a health condition or disability that makes it difficult for them to do normal things, they have an infirmity.

"Likewise the Spirit also helpeth our infirmities [illnesses]" (Romans 8:26).

Inheritance: the passing down of land, money, or belongings to an heir. It's like when a grandparent, parent, or other family member leaves behind money, property, or possessions to their loved ones in their will.

"Unto these the land shall be divided for an inheritance [passing down to an heir]" (Numbers 26:53).

Moses and the Ten Commandments

Iniquity: sin, wickedness, or evil; something that is morally or ethically wrong. When someone steals money from the company they work for, they have committed iniquity.

"And after all that is come upon us for our evil deeds, and for our great trespass, seeing that thou our God hast punished us less than our iniquities [sins] deserve, and hast given us such deliverance as this" (Ezra 9:13).

Innocent: free from sin, guilt, or moral wrong. To be innocent is the opposite of guilty. In a court of law, the jury listens to evidence and determines if a person is innocent or guilty.

"Because I am innocent [free from sin], surely his anger shall turn from me" (Jeremiah 2:35).

Instruction: training, education, or teaching provided to help someone learn. It's like when a parent provides directions, explanations, or demonstrations to help a child learn to tie their shoes.

"Apply thine heart unto instruction [training], and thine ears to the words of knowledge" (Proverbs 23:12).

Integrity: the quality of having a good moral character; upright or honest. For instance, when someone acts in a way that is consistent with their values and beliefs, even when no one is watching.

"Till I die I will not remove mine integrity [good moral character] from me" (Job 27:5).

Israel: another name for the Old Testament prophet Jacob, his family, and his descendants. According to the Bible, the Jewish people today are descendants of Israel (Jacob).

"For, lo, I will command, and I will sift the house of Israel [Jacob's family and descendants] among all nations" (Amos 9:9).

Jealous: the feeling of being unhappy or resentful because someone has something that you want. Jealousy is a synonym for envy. It's like when you feel upset or envious because someone else has something that you wish you had.

"Then will the Lord be jealous [envious] for his land, and pity his people" (Joel 2:18).

Jehovah: the Old Testament name for the God of Israel. Jehovah is considered a sacred name to both Christian and Jewish faiths.

"That men may know that thou, whose name alone is JEHOVAH [God], art the most high over all the earth" (Psalm 83:18).

Joined: when parts have been united or fastened together. For example, you can join puzzle pieces together, piece by piece, to create a larger picture.

"For this cause shall a man leave his father and mother, and shall be joined [united] unto his wife" (Ephesians 5:31).

Jot: the smallest Hebrew letter ("i"). In the Bible, Jesus refers to the jot to explain that God is aware of and will take care of the many small details in bringing about His work.

"For verily I say unto you, Till heaven and earth pass, one jot [small letter] or one tittle shall in no wise pass from the law, till all be fulfilled" (Matthew 5:18).

Joy: gladness, delight; a sense of pleasure or contentment that comes from within. It's like when you feel really happy or excited about something, and it makes you feel good on the inside.

"I bring you good tidings of great joy [gladness]" (Luke 2:10).

Judge: Definition 1: a person who decides if someone is guilty of breaking the law (or commandments) and if they should be punished. A judge presides in a courtroom of law.

"But he that did his neighbour wrong thrust him away, saying, Who made thee a ruler and a judge [person deciding if we broke the commandments] over us?" (Acts 7:27).

Judge: Definition 2: to form an opinion about someone or something; to criticize. For example, when a friend says they don't like to eat vegetables, and you criticize them, you are judging them.

"Judge [form opinions] not, that ye be not judged [criticized]" (Matthew 7:1).

Just: morally upright or righteous in the eyes of God. It's like when something is done or decided in a way that is fair and impartial, treating everyone equally and without bias.

"The way of the just [righteous] is uprightness" (Isaiah 26:7).

Justified: to be forgiven or be made blameless; to make exact. According to the Bible, being justified is made possible by the Atonement of Jesus Christ.

"Therefore being justified [forgiven] by faith, we have peace with God through our Lord Jesus Christ" (Romans 5:1).

Keeper: a person in charge of someone or something. Types of keepers include a zoo keeper, who takes care of animals in a zoo; a goal keeper, who protects the goal in soccer; and a warden, who manages prisoners in a jail.

"And the keeper [warden] of the prison awaking out of his sleep, and seeing the prison doors open, he drew out his sword" (Acts 16:27).

Key: a tool used for opening locks, such as in a door. Usually, a person has several keys used to unlock things like their home, car, or a bike lock.

"For ye have taken away the key [tool to unlock] of knowledge" (Luke 11:52).

Kid: a young goat. Goat kids are smaller and more playful than adult goats, and they are often raised on farms for their milk, meat, or as pets.

"And they took Joseph's coat, and killed a kid [young goat] of the goats" (Genesis 37:31).

Kin: someone who is a family member or a relative. Kin includes relatives such as parents, siblings, grandparents, aunts, uncles, and cousins, among others.

"None of you shall approach to any that is near of kin [family member] to him" (Leviticus 18:6).

Kindness: to act with consideration, generosity, and thoughtfulness. For example, when a parent patiently helps a child with their homework, they are acting with kindness.

"But with everlasting kindness [consideration] will I have mercy on thee" (Isaiah 54:8).

Kindred: a person's tribe, lineage, or family. Your kindred are people who are connected to you through family ties and who share your ancestry, heritage, or genealogy.

"Ye are the children of the prophets, and of the covenant which God made with our fathers, saying unto Abraham, And in thy seed shall all the kindreds [families] of the earth be blessed" (Acts 3:25).

Kingdom: a monarchical form of government for an empire or nation where a king or queen holds supreme power. In the Bible, prophets teach that eventually the Lord will reign over the earth like a monarch.

"Thine is the kingdom [empire], O Lord, and thou art exalted as head above all" (1 Chronicles 29:11).

Knock: to summon by making a sound on a door; to call. When we hear knocking on a door, we typically go to see who is there and what they need.

"Behold, I stand at the door, and knock [summon you]: if any man hear my voice, and open the door, I will come in to him, and will sup with him, and he with me" (Revelation 3:20).

Know: to perceive, be familiar with, or have learned information. For example, you might "know" the answer to a math problem, "know" the capital of a country, or "know" how to ride a bike.

"For God doth know [perceive] that in the day ye eat thereof" (Genesis 3:5).

Labour: to work or effort on a task or project. For instance, household chores, school assignments, and other tasks that require effort and work can be considered "labour."

"Come unto me, all ye that labour [work] and are heavy laden" (Matthew 11:28).

Lack: when there is a need, a shortage, or someone in want of something necessary or desired. For example, if you say that you "lack" money, it means that you do not have enough money to meet your needs or desires.

"And that ye may have lack [need] of nothing" (1 Thessalonians 4:12).

Laden: someone or something that is burdened, loaded, or weighted down. When a tree with branches weighed down by a heavy layer of snow might be described as "laden."

"Come unto me, all ye that labour and are heavy laden [burdened]" (Matthew 11:28).

Lamb: a young sheep less than a year old. In Old Testament times lambs were sacrificed as part of the repentance process, a practice that foreshadowed and symbolized the sacrifice of Jesus.

"He is brought as a lamb [young sheep] to the slaughter" (Isaiah 53:7).

Lame: a person unable to walk due to injury, disease, or weakness. For example, if a person has a sprained ankle, they might walk with a limp and be described as "lame."

"If ye offer the lame [person unable to walk] and sick, is it not evil?" (Malachi 1:8).

Lament: to show sorrow, sadness, or grief. For example, people might lament the destruction caused by a hurricane or express lamentation over the loss of lives in a war.

"Or this gird you with sackcloth, lament [show sorrow] and howl" (Jeremiah 4:8).

Lasciviousness: wanton, indecent, or unruly behavior, often involving a lack of restraint or modesty. Lascivious behavior is generally considered inappropriate and goes against social norms and expectations of proper conduct, especially in formal or public settings.

"Turning the grace of our God into lasciviousness [indecent behavior]" (Jude 1:4).

Latchet: the strap or thong of a sandal or shoe. For example, the part of a shoe that holds the laces together and allows you to adjust the tightness of the shoe is called the latchet.

"Nor the latchet [strap] of their shoes be broken" (Isaiah 5:27).

Lawful: something that is legal or allowed by the law. In the Bible, the Mosaic Law was used to govern people's behavior and was especially restrictive on the sabbath.

"It is the sabbath day: it is not lawful [legal] for thee to carry thy bed" (John 5:10).

Laying on of Hands: a religious practice where someone with priesthood authority places their hands on another person (typically the head) and prays for them. In Christianity, laying on of hands is typically how confirmation (gift of the Holy Ghost) is given.

"And when they had prayed, they laid their hands [confirmation] on them" (Acts 6:6).

Lay up: to store away or build up a supply of something. When a person puts money in a savings account to use for emergencies, they are laying up a supply of money.

"Therefore shall ye lay up (store) these my words in your heart and in your soul, and bind them for a sign upon your hand" (Deuteronomy 11:18).

League: alliance, pact, or partnership formed between a group of people or organizations. For example, a sports league is a group of teams that compete against each other in organized games or competitions, such as a soccer league or a baseball league.

"We be come from a far country: now therefore make ye a league [alliance] with us" (Joshua 9:6).

Least: lowest or smallest person or thing in power or position. When a dog has puppies and one is smaller than the others, it might be described as the "least."

"I am the least [lowest in position] in my father's house" (Judges 6:15).

Leaven: to raise or lighten bread through fermentation of yeast. In the Bible, yeast or leavening is sometimes used as a symbol of being prideful or puffed up.

"It shall not be baken with leaven [yeast]" (Leviticus 6:17).

Legion: a battalion of Roman soldiers, usually 3,000 to 6,000 men. Legion is also sometimes used in the Bible to mean a large number, such as a legion of angels or a legion of demons.

"My name is Legion [battalion of soldiers]: for we are many" (Mark 5:9).

Leper: a person suffering from the scaly disease of leprosy. In Bible times, lepers were considered unclean and were cast out of society for fear of being contagious.

"This shall be the law of the leper [person with leprosy] in the day of his cleansing" (Leviticus 14:2).

Leprosy: a contagious disease caused by bacteria, which affects the skin and nerves and can lead to deformities if untreated. In modern times, leprosy is called Hansen's disease and is considered curable.

"Take heed in the plague of leprosy [contagious disease], that thou observe diligently" (Deuteronomy 24:8).

Lest: taking action to prevent a negative outcome; for fear that. For example, "He studied hard lest he fail the test" means that he studied hard to prevent the possibility of failing the test.

"And the foolish said unto the wise, Give us of your oil; for our lamps are gone out. But the wise answered, saying, Not so; lest [we are afraid that] there be not enough for us and you" (Matthew 25:8-9).

Levite: a person from the Tribe of Levi, which officiated in the Aaronic priesthood. Levites performed lesser services during public worship services, such as being musicians, gatekeepers, or guardians.

"The Jews sent priests and Levites [Aaronic priesthood holders] from Jerusalem to ask him" (John 1:19).

Liar: someone who is dishonest, or who tells lies. For example, if someone says they didn't eat the last cookie when they actually did, they would be considered a liar.

"A poor man is better than a liar [a dishonest person]" (Proverbs 19:22).

Liken: to make a comparison. "He likened the taste of the fruit to that of a tropical paradise," means that he compared the taste of the fruit to the idea of a tropical paradise.

"Whereunto shall we liken [compare to] the kingdom of God?" (Mark 4:30).

Likeness: a similarity in shape or looks that shows a resemblance to someone or something. An artist who paints a portrait of someone is hoping to catch a likeness of them so others will see the resemblance.

"And took upon him the form of a servant, and was made in the likeness [similarity in shape] of men" (Philippians 2:7).

Locust: a type of grasshopper, or large legged insect known for mass migration and destroying crops. In the Old Testament, one of the ten plagues of Egypt was locusts that ate the crops.

"That which the palmerworm hath left hath the locust [grasshopper] eaten; and that which the locust [grasshopper] hath left hath the cankerworm eaten" (Joel 1:4).

Loins: the lower back; hips and waist. The term "loins" is also used in some expressions to refer to strength, power, or vitality, such as in "gird up your loins."

"Stand therefore, having your loins [lower back] girt about with truth, and having on the breastplate of righteousness" (Ephesians 6:14).

Long-Suffering: the quality of having patient endurance and persistence. For example, a person who remains calm and patient while waiting in a long line, dealing with a difficult person, or facing a prolonged illness, could be described as long-suffering.

"By pureness, by knowledge, by longsuffering [patient endurance]" (2 Corinthians 6:6).

Loose: to untie, set free, or allow movement. When your shoe comes untied, or when your dog escapes the back yard, it could be described as loose. Past tense: loosed.

"Whatsoever thou shalt loose [untie] on earth shall be loosed [untied] in heaven" (Matthew 16:19).

Lucre: wealth or money earned from a dishonorable source. For instance, "He was accused of amassing lucre through deceitful activities" means that he was accused of gaining money through dishonest or deceitful methods.

"Not given to wine, no striker, not greedy of filthy lucre [money]; but patient, not a brawler, not covetous" (1 Timothy 3:3).

Magician: a person who practices magic or sorcery. Magicians are often skilled entertainers who use sleight of hand, misdirection, and other techniques to create seemingly impossible or mysterious effects, such as making objects disappear, levitate, or change form.

"And the magicians [people who practiced magic] could not stand before Moses because of the boils" (Exodus 9:11).

Magistrate: a justice of the peace or city officer who helps ensure laws are enforced. Usually, magistrates have the power to issue warrants, conduct hearings, make rulings, and impose penalties or fines within the scope of their jurisdiction.

"When thou goest with thine adversary to the magistrate [justice of the peace], as thou art in the way" (Luke 12:58).

Magnify: to glorify; to speak or act for the glory or honor of someone or something. When you announce on social media and celebrate the accomplishments of someone who has succeeded, you are magnifying them to others.

"For they heard them speak with tongues, and magnify [glorify] God" (Acts 10:46).

Maimed: someone or something that has been severely injured or disabled, typically resulting in the loss of a body part and becoming significantly impaired. A person who has to have a leg amputated might be described as maimed.

"But when thou makest a feast, call the poor, the maimed [injured], the lame, the blind" (Luke 14:13).

Majesty: the greatness, dignity, or noble nature of someone or something. It can be used to describe the regal or formal demeanor of a king or queen, or the imposing presence of a mountain.

"But were eyewitnesses of his majesty [greatness]" (2 Peter 1:16).

Maker: someone who is a creator; name for God or Christ. In the Bible, during the Creation of the Earth, God shows both His control over all things and His authority over all the universe as the Maker.

"He that oppresseth the poor reproacheth his Maker [Creator]" (Proverbs 14:31).

Malice: the desire to harm another person. Someone who purposefully trips another person, hoping they will fall, could be described as behaving with malice.

Jesus heals the blind man.

"Howbeit in malice [desire to harm others] be ye children, but in understanding be men" (1 Corinthians 14:20).

Mammon: the desire for wealth, riches, or worldly things. According to the Bible, a person who pursues mammon or worldly things is practicing a form of idolatry.

"Make to yourselves friends of the mammon [worldliness] of unrighteousness" (Luke 16:9).

Manifest: to demonstrate or show something so it becomes clear to others. For example, a person's happiness may manifest in their smile.

"This beginning of miracles did Jesus in Cana of Galilee, and manifested [demonstrated] forth his glory; and his disciples believed on him" (John 2:11).

Mankind: a word used to describe all of humanity, both men and women and those from all cultures. Mankind is used to refer to the entire human race.

"For whoremongers, for them that defile themselves with mankind [humans]" (1 Timothy 1:10).

Manna: a food supplied miraculously to the Israelites after the Exodus while they traveled through the wilderness. In the New Testament, the apostle John called it "bread from heaven" (John 6:31).

"Our fathers did eat manna [food] in the desert" (John 6:31).

Manner: an old-fashioned word that refers to the kind of, sort or, or type of something. Someone who asks, "What manner of dog is that?" is asking what type or kind of dog it is.
"What manner [kind] of persons ought ye to be" (2 Peter 3:11).

Mantle: a sleeveless cloak, usually worn loose as an outer layer over the clothes. It was often draped over the shoulders like a shawl. Mantles were often worn for warmth or to show status.

"And when he had turned in unto her into the tent, she covered him with a mantle [sleeveless cloak]" (Judges 4:18).

Marrow: soft, spongy tissue that is inmost or in the center part of a bone. Marrow is responsible for producing red blood cells, white blood cells, and platelets, which are essential to the body.

"It shall be health to thy navel, and marrow [soft tissue] to thy bones" (Proverbs 3:8).

Martyr: a person willing to suffer punishment or death to support a cause, belief, or principle they believe in. In the Bible, many of the 12 Apostles became martyrs, including Peter, Paul, James, and Stephen.

"And when the blood of thy martyr [victim of persecution and death] Stephen was shed, I also was standing by" (Acts 22:20).

Measure: the process of judging, determining, or comparing the size (length, weight), amount, or degree of something. When a person takes measure of damage done after a flood, they are judging how much damage occurred.

"With what measure [judgment] ye mete, it shall be measured [judged] to you again" (Matthew 7:2).

Mediator: a person, sometimes called an intermediary, who helps two people resolve an argument and come together. In the Bible, mediator is sometimes used as a name for Jesus Christ.

"By how much also he is the mediator [intermediary] of a better covenant" (Hebrews 8:6).

Meek: a word used to describe someone who is humble, gentle, or self-restrained. In the Old Testament, Job behaved meekly when he patiently submitted and refused to be angry with the Lord for his many trials.

"The meek [humble] will he guide in judgment: and the meek [humble] will he teach his way" (Psalm 25:9).

Meet: an older word used describe something that is agreeable, fits, or suitable. For example, a warm coat is meet for cold weather, a sharp knife is meet for cutting food, and a quiet room is meet for studying.

"Bring forth therefore fruits meet [fit] for repentance" (Matthew 3:8).

Mercy: to show kindness or give grace to someone who has done something wrong or is in a difficult situation. Someone might show mercy by helping a stranger in need. Mercy is often used as a synonym for forgiveness.

"O give thanks unto the Lord; for he is good; for his mercy [forgiveness] endureth for ever" (1 Chronicles 16:34).

Messiah: an Aramaic word that means "the anointed." In the Bible, Messiah is a name that refers to the Savior of the world.

"Know therefore and understand, that from the going forth of the commandment to restore and to build Jerusalem unto the Messiah [Savior] the Prince shall be seven weeks" (Daniel 9:25).

Midst: a word that refers to the middle, interior, or center of something. For example, a person standing in the midst of a crowd is standing in the middle of the crowd.

"And I saw another angel fly in the midst [middle] of heaven" (Revelation 14:6).

Mighty: term used to describe someone or something that is of great ability, strength, or power. For example, a mighty athlete is someone who is strong and powerful.

"Seeing that Abraham shall surely become a great and mighty [great] nation" (Genesis 18:18).

Millstone: a large cylindrical stone used in a mill for grinding grain. Millstones measured as large as six feet in diameter and were rotated by livestock to crush grain.

"And a certain woman cast a piece of a millstone [large stone] upon Abimelech's head" (Judges 9:53).

Minister: a religious leader who guides and advises people on spiritual matters and gives service to those in need. Martin Luther King, Jr. was a famous minister who worked to promote civil rights in the 1950-60s.

"Yet they shall be ministers [religious leaders] in my sanctuary, having charge at the gates of the house, and ministering [giving service] to the house" (Ezekiel 44:11).

Mire: a place with deep mud or swampy wetlands. For example, a car stuck in mud is said to be in a mire.

"The dog is turned to his own vomit again; and the sow that was washed to her wallowing in the mire [mud]" (2 Peter 2:22).

Mirth: a feeling of happiness, merriment, or joy that is expressed through laughter or cheerfulness. For instance, the sound of children's laughter in a playground can be described as mirthful.

"And all the people went their way to eat, and to drink, and to send portions, and to make great mirth [merriment]" (Nehemiah 8:12).

Mischief: behavior that is playful or mischievous, but can also be harmful or troublesome. When someone plays an April Fool's prank on someone, they are engaging in mischief.

"Mischief [harm] shall come upon mischief [harm], and rumour shall be upon rumour" (Ezekiel 7:26).

Mist of Darkness: a fog that is symbolic of Satan's presence. According to the scriptures, those lost in the mist of darkness are being tempted by Satan.

"To whom the mist of darkness [Satan's presence] is reserved for ever" (2 Peter 2:17).

Mock: behavior that is meant to make fun of or tease someone in a harmful, sarcastic way. If someone is mimicking or harassing another person in a way that is meant to make them feel bad, they are mocking them.

"Fools make a mock [make fun of] at sin" (Proverbs 14:9).

Molten: something that is made by melting metal and pouring it into a mold for shaping. Molten processes are often used in trades, such as metalworking or glassblowing.

"For his molten [molded] image is falsehood" (Jeremiah 10:14).

Morrow: an old-fashioned term used to describe the next day or the day after. If someone says "I'll see you tomorrow," they mean they will see the person the following day, or on the morrow.

"Take therefore no thought for the morrow [tomorrow]: for the morrow [tomorrow] shall take thought for the things of itself" (Matthew 6:34).

Mote: a small particle of something, often too small to be seen with the naked eye. For example, dust particles floating in the air can be described as motes.

"Why beholdest thou the mote [small particle] that is in thy brother's eye" (Matthew 7:3).

Multiply: a process of increasing, flourishing, or getting larger or bigger. In the Bible, the Lord commands Adam and Eve to "multiply", meaning to have children and increase the size of their family.

"And in multiplying [increasing] I will multiply [increase] thy seed as the stars of the heaven" (Genesis 22:17).

Multitude: a crowd, or a great number of people or things. For example, a multitude of people might gather at a concert or a festival.

"Great multitudes [crowds] followed him, and he healed them all" (Matthew 12:15).

Murmur: term used to complaint expressed softly under their breath. For example, people might murmur to each other during a quiet conversation so that others don't hear they are not happy.

"Neither murmur [complain] ye, as some of them also murmured [complained]" (1 Corinthians 10:10).

Myrrh: a sacred anointing oil made from tree resin. Myrrh has been used for thousands of years for its fragrance and medicinal properties.

"And they gave him to drink wine mingled with myrrh [anointing oil]: but he received it not" (Mark 15:23).

Nakedness: the condition of being nude, bare, or without clothes. In the Bible, nakedness is sometimes used symbolically to represent being exposed or having our sins seen by God.

"Thy nakedness [nudity] shall be uncovered, yea, thy shame shall be seen" (Isaiah 47:3).

Natural: an individual who is guided by their basic instincts and impulses, rather than trying to live in obedience to the commandments. In the Bible, natural sometimes refers to the fallen state of humans after Adam and Eve were forced to leave the Garden of Eden.

"But the natural [fallen] man receiveth not the things of the Spirit of God" (1 Corinthians 2:14).

Necessity: something that is required or essential, either to life or as required by law. For example, food, water, and shelter are all necessities of life.

"For of necessity [required by law] he must release one unto them at the feast" (Luke 23:17).

Needful: an adjective that describes when something is necessary, useful, or indispensable. For example, if a student wants to do well on an exam, studying is needful.

"Notwithstanding ye give them not those things which are needful [necessary] to the body; what doth it profit?" (James 2:16).

Needy: an adjective that describes very poor people or those in want of basic necessities or care. Needy individuals are often unable to provide for themselves due to poverty, illness, disability, or other circumstances.

"For the needy [very poor people] shall not alway be forgotten" (Psalm 9:18).

Neglect: to treat carelessly or without necessary attention to. When a pet owner goes on vacation without arranging care for their animal, they are treating it with neglect.

"Neglect [treat carelessly] not the gift that is in thee" (1 Timothy 4:14).

Neighbour: a person who lives or dwells nearby. Often neighbors can be helpful in many ways, like watching your house when you're away, borrowing a cup of sugar, or playing games with you.

"Take ye heed every one of his neighbour [person living nearby]" (Jeremiah 9:4).

Nigh: something that is near, close together, or adjacent. It can be used to describe a physical distance or a length of time. For example, if your house is nigh to the park, it means that the park is located very close to your house.

"This people draweth nigh [near] unto me with their mouth, and honoureth me with their lips; but their heart is far from me" (Matthew 15:8).

Noble: a person with high social or political status. A noble might come from a royal or aristocratic family. For example, a prince or princess would be considered as noble.

"By me princes rule, and nobles [people with social or political status], even all the judges of the earth" (Proverbs 8:16).

Noised: to make something known or to spread by rumor. When someone says that the accident was "noised among all the class," they mean that it was talked about and made known to everyone in the class.

"So the Lord was with Joshua; and his fame was noised [made known] throughout all the country" (Joshua 6:27).

Nought: meaning nothing, none, or zero. It can also mean a situation where there is no value or significance. For example, when someone says, "it came to nought," they mean that something has failed or ended without any success or result.

"For thus saith the Lord, Ye have sold yourselves for nought [nothing]; and ye shall be redeemed without money" (Isaiah 52:3).

Nourish: the act of feeding or giving a person, animal, or plant the nutrients they need to live or promote growth and well-being. For example, the chicken soup nourished Sue back to health when she suffered from a cold.

"And there will I nourish [feed] thee; for yet there are five years of famine" (Genesis 45:11).

Oath: a sacred promise to tell the truth or do a certain thing. When taking an oath, a person might place their hand on the Bible or raise their right hand to show they are making a solemn promise.

"They clave to their brethren, their nobles, and entered into a curse, and into an oath [sacred promise], to walk in God's law, which was given by Moses the servant of God" (Nehemiah 10:29).

Obedience: to follow rules, commands, or laws. For instance, when you follow the rules at school, you are being obedient and helping everyone have a good learning experience.

"By whom we have received grace and apostleship, for obedience [follow the rules] to the faith" (Romans 1:5).

Oblation: a religious term that refers to a sacrifice or offering given to God. In the Old Testament, oblations were part of a ritual or ceremony, where the offerings were made in a specific way or at a specific time.

"We have therefore brought an oblation [sacrifice] for the Lord, what every man hath gotten, of jewels of gold, chains, and bracelets, rings, earrings, and tablets, to make an atonement for our souls before the Lord" (Numbers 31:50).

Obscurity: something that is not well known or understood. Obscurity can be used as a synonym for darkness, or a lack of understanding.

"We wait for light, but behold obscurity [darkness]; for brightness" (Isaiah 59:9).

Observe: an old-fashioned word for being obedient or following guidelines. If your teacher at school asks you to observe the rules, they are asking you to be obedient.

"Whoso is wise, and will observe [obeying] these things" (Psalm 107:43).

Offering: a gift or sacrifice made to the Lord. Offerings can be physical items, such as money, food, or flowers; or it can be giving service to someone in need.

"For all these have of their abundance cast in unto the offerings [gifts] of God" (Luke 21:4).

Officer: a priesthood holder or person in authority. In the Bible, Abraham traveled to pay his tithing to Melchizedek, who was the King of Salem and the high priest, or an officer in the priesthood.

"Judges and officers [priesthood holders] shalt thou make thee in all thy gates" (Deuteronomy 16:18).

Offspring: the children or descendants of a particular parent or family. For example, in the Bible Adam and Eve had several offspring, including Cain, Able, and Seth.

"I am the root and the offspring [descendant] of David" (Revelation 22:16).

Ointment: a medicinal cream or salve applied to the skin to help soothe, heal, or protect it. Ointments are often used to treat skin conditions, such as dry skin, rashes, and infections.

"Let thy head lack no ointment [medicinal cream]" (Ecclesiastes 9:8).

Omega: the last letter of the Greek alphabet, which is often used to represent the end of something. In the Bible, God is referred to as Alpha and Omega because He is eternal and has no beginning or end.

"I am Alpha and Omega [end], the beginning and the ending" (Revelation 1:8).

Oppress: to treat someone or a group of people in a cruel or unjust manner, often by using power or authority to burden, control, or exploit them. For example, people who are forced into slavery are being oppressed.

"Ye shall not therefore oppress [exploit] one another; but thou shalt fear thy God" (Leviticus 25:17).

Oracle: a prophet or messenger from God. Isaiah, Jeremiah, and Ezekiel are just a few of the oracles or prophets whose writings are found in the Old Testament.

"If any man speak, let him speak as the oracles [prophets] of God" (1 Peter 4:11).

Ordain: to give someone priesthood authority, or to place a person in a religious leadership position. The process of ordination usually involves a formal ceremony using the laying on of hands and prayer.

"I ordained [gave priesthood authority to] thee a prophet unto the nations" (Jeremiah 1:5).

Ordinance: a sacred ceremony, such as baptism, where a person promises to follow God's commandments. Other ordinances in Christianity include communion (sacrament), confirmation, anointing with oil, marriage, healing the sick.

"That they may walk in my statutes, and keep mine ordinances [promises made to keep commandments], and do them: and they shall be my people, and I will be their God" (Ezekiel 11:20).

Ought: a word that means "should" or that there is a moral or ethical duty to do something. For example, we might say that we ought to be honest, or we ought to treat people with kindness.

The Parable of the Good Samaritan

"Seeing then that all these things shall be dissolved, what manner of persons ought [should] ye to be in all holy conversation and godliness . . .?" (2 Peter 3:11).

Outcast: a rejected person; someone who is cast out or exiled, usually because they are seen as different, undesirable, or have broken a law. In the Old Testament, Jephthah became an outcast because his mother was a prostitute.

"And he shall set up an ensign for the nations, and shall assemble the outcasts [rejected people] of Israel" (Isaiah 11:12).

Outward: the external, visible, or outside appearance of something. When you look at the outward appearance of a person, you are looking at their clothing, their hair, and face.

"For man looketh on the outward [outside] appearance, but the Lord looketh on the heart" (1 Samuel 16:7).

Overcome: to successfully deal with, to conquer, or to defeat a challenge or obstacle. For example, when someone overcomes an addiction, they can live a healthy life without relying on what they were previously addicted to. Past tense: overcame.

"Be of good cheer; I have overcome [conquered] the world" (John 16:33).

Oversight: the act of monitoring or supervising something to ensure it is managed well and done correctly. A mayor, for example, is responsible for the oversight of the government in their city.

"Into the hands of them that did the work, that had the oversight [supervision] of the house of the Lord" (2 Kings 12:11).

Owe: to be in debt for something, or to have to repay someone for something they have done for you. If a person agrees to pay money to get their house painted, they owe the painter that money when the job is completed.

"Owe [be in debt for] no man any thing, but to love one another" (Romans 13:8).

Pacify: to make peace with someone, especially when they are upset or angry. For example, if your little sister is crying because she lost a toy, you might try to pacify her with a hug.

"But a wise man will pacify [make peace with] it" (Proverbs 16:14).

Palsy: a medical condition that causes shaking, weakness, and loss of muscle control. A person with palsy might have trouble speaking, walking, or may even be paralyzed.

"Lord, my servant lieth at home sick of the palsy [disabled], grievously tormented" (Matthew 8:6).

Parable: a short story that has a moral or meaning to it. For instance, the story of "The Tortoise and the Hare" is a parable that teaches diligence in the face of difficulty.

"Now learn a parable [short story] of the fig tree" (Mark 13:28).

Paradise: a place of great beauty, like a dream world where everyone is happy and blissful. In the Bible, the Garden of Eden was a paradise.

"To day shalt thou be with me in paradise [a place of great beauty]" (Luke 23:43).

Pardon: to forgive a wrongdoing and not hold it against the person anymore. Government leaders, like the president, have the authority to grant pardons to prisoners.

"I pray thee, pardon [forgive] my sin, and turn again with me" (1 Samuel 15:25).

Passover: a Jewish celebration in memory of the deliverance of the Israelites from slavery in ancient Egypt. It is called Passover because God "passed over" the houses of the Israelites and spared them from the tenth plague, which killed the firstborns of the Egyptians.

"The Master saith, My time is at hand; I will keep the passover [religious celebration] at thy house with my disciples" (Matthew 26:18).

Pastor: a spiritual guide, minister, or elder who guides and supports members of a congregation. The word pastor comes from a Latin word which means "shepherd."

"Woe be unto the pastors [spiritual guides] that destroy and scatter the sheep of my pasture" (Jeremiah 23:1).

Pasture: a field or land covered with grass or vegetation eaten by grazing animals. In a pasture, the animals can roam freely and eat grass and other vegetation that grows there.

"He maketh me to lie down in green pastures [fields]" (Psalm 23:2).

Patience: the ability to wait calmly for something to happen. Patience requires self-restraint, even when things might get difficult.

"Knowing that tribulation worketh patience [self-restraint]" (Romans 5:3).

Patriarch: the male leader of a family (a father) or community. Abraham, Isaac, and Jacob are three well-respected patriarchs of the House of Israel who are respected in the Bible.

"Let me freely speak unto you of the patriarch [father] David" (Acts 2:29).

Peace: a state of harmony, tranquility, or freedom from conflict or war. When people live in peace, they can work together to solve problems and are happier.

"And in this place will I give peace [harmony]" (Haggai 2:9).

Peculiar: something that is special, uncommon, or different, making it stand out. For example, a person might have a peculiar habit or way of speaking that is different from others.

"If ye will obey my voice indeed, and keep my covenant, then ye shall be a peculiar [special] treasure unto me" (Exodus 19:5).

Pence: a form of currency that is equal to one penny in British pound sterling (money). If a person has only one pence, they have very little money.

"When he departed, he took out two pence [pennies], and gave them to the host" (Luke 10:35).

Perfect: the condition of being complete, flawless, or ideal. For instance, a perfect score on a test means that all the answers are correct and there are no mistakes.

"Thou shalt be perfect [complete] with the Lord thy God" (Deuteronomy 18:13).

Peril: a situation that involves danger or risk. When someone walks along the edge of a cliff they are in peril of falling off.

"We gat our bread with the peril [danger] of our lives because of the sword of the wilderness" (Lamentations 5:9).

Perish: to die or be destroyed. When something perishes, it is no longer useful or has come to an end.

"And his disciples came to him, and awoke him, saying, Lord, save us: we perish [die]" (Matthew 8:25).

Perpetual: something that goes on indefinitely, unceasingly, or is continuous. When the sun always shines on a tropical island, it might be described as perpetually sunny.

"For it is their perpetual [unending] possession" (Leviticus 25:34).

Perverse: the behavior of those who choose to do things that are wicked, harmful, or corrupt. For example, a driver who deliberately runs red lights and breaks the speed limit might be described as perverse.

"In the midst of a crooked and perverse [wicked] nation" (Philippians 2:15).

Pestilence: a contagious disease, like a plague, that leads to sickness and possibly death. The bubonic plague in the Middle Ages is an example of a pestilence.

"I will send the pestilence [disease] among you" (Leviticus 26:25).

Petition: to ask for in a formal way, or to plead for something greatly needed. For instance, a person might petition the city council to build a park in their neighborhood.

"Then she said, I desire one small petition [plead for] of thee" (1 Kings 2:20).

Pity: to show kindness, generosity, or mercy toward another person who is in distress. For example, you might feel pity for a homeless person sleeping on the street.

"Shouldest not thou also have had compassion on thy fellowservant, even as I had pity [generosity] on thee?" (Matthew 18:33).

Plague: a widespread deadly infectious disease that impacts many people. The Covid-19 pandemic is considered one of the world's deadliest plagues on record.

"The Lord smote the people with a very great plague [widespread sickness]" (Numbers 11:33).

Plaited: something that has been braided or woven together. For example, a braid in someone's hair is a plaited hairstyle.

"And when they had plaited [braided] a crown of thorns, they put it upon his head" (Matthew 27:29).

Pluck: to pull something out of or off from something, like feathers, hair, or such. When a woman plucks her eyebrows, it means she is pulling some of the hairs out of them.

"And began to pluck [pull] the ears of corn, and to eat" (Matthew 12:1).

Pollute: to contaminate, make unclean, or defile something pure. When a car emits exhaust, it pollutes the air and can cause smog.

"And they shall pollute [make unclean] the sanctuary of strength" (Daniel 11:31).

Ponder: to think deeply about something or to meditate. If you ponder a question or a problem, you are reflecting on it carefully to try and find an answer.

"Ponder [think about] the path of thy feet, and let all thy ways be established" (Proverbs 4:26).

Poor in Spirit or Heart: the condition of being meek or humble. A person who is poor in spirit is ready to repent and get baptized.

"Blessed are the poor in spirit [humble]" (Matthew 5:3).

Portion: a part or piece of the whole of something. For example, a portion of a pizza might be a slice that has been cut from the whole pizza.

"And the Lord shall inherit Judah his portion [part] in the holy land" (Zechariah 2:12).

Posterity: a person's children, grandchildren, and descendants. According to the Bible, the people living on Earth today are the posterity of Adam and Eve.

"Let his posterity [children and grandchildren] be cut off" (Psalm 109:13).

Pray: to communicate or speak with God. Praying can involve speaking out loud or silently, and may include specific behaviors like kneeling, bowing the head, or folding arms.

"If my people, which are called by my name, shall humble themselves, and pray [speak with God]" (2 Chronicles 7:14).

Precept: a commandment or wisdom given to help people know what to do. For instance, a precept in a classroom might be to "treat others the way you want to be treated."

"For when Moses had spoken every precept [commandment] to all the people according to the law" (Hebrews 9:19).

Preeminence: the position of being the best, greatest, or superior. For example, a company that has preeminence in a particular industry is one that is widely recognized as being the best.

"That in all things he might have the preeminence [best]" (Colossians 1:18).

Prevail: to succeed, or to strongly influence or persuade someone to do something, especially in challenging circumstances. When someone overcomes a difficult obstacle or challenge, we can say that they have prevailed.

"The gates of hell shall not prevail [succeed] against it" (Matthew 16:18).

Prey: an animal that is hunted for food; or a person weak in spirit who is tempted by Satan. A worm might be the prey of a bird, and a mouse might be the prey of a cat.

"Have they not sped? have they not divided the prey [hunted animals]" (Judges 5:30).

Pride: to boast or have an unreasonable sense of self-esteem and a lack of humility. The Bible warns against excessive pride and conceit, which can lead to downfall and destruction.

"And I will break the pride [boastfulness] of your power" (Leviticus 26:19).

Priesthood: the authority to act in God's name, or power given from God. In the Old Testament, the Aaronic priesthood was reserved for the descendants of Aaron, who was the brother of Moses.

"For their anointing shall surely be an everlasting priesthood [authority] throughout their generations" (Exodus 40:15).

Principality: a government ruled by a prince, king, or monarchy. For example, the Bible speaks of the "principality of Persia" (see Daniel 10:13), a powerful empire in its day.

"Far above all principality [government], and power, and might, and dominion" (Ephesians 1:21).

Privily: an old-fashioned word that means to do something secretly or without others knowing. In the Bible, Judas Iscariot betrayed Jesus privily.

"Then Joseph her husband, being a just man, and not willing to make her a publick example, was minded to put her away privily [secretly]" (Matthew 1:19).

Profane: behavior that is disrespectful toward God or holy things. A person who disobeys God's commands or violates religious rituals might be described as profane.

"Thou hast despised mine holy things, and hast profaned [been disrespectful toward] my sabbaths" (Ezekiel 22:8).

Profit: to gain, benefit, or earn a positive return on investment. In the Bible, a profit refers to the benefit or gain that comes from following God's commands and living a righteous life, instead of money.

"Treasures of wickedness profit [benefit] nothing" (Proverbs 10:2).

Proof: the evidence of truth. For example, in a court of law, the prosecution may present proof that a defendant committed a crime.

"Wherefore shew ye to them, and before the churches, the proof [evidence] of your love" (2 Corinthians 8:24).

Prophesy: truth, warning, or inspiration given by God to a prophet. Prophesy can also refer to the act of delivering these messages from God.

"And the Lord said unto me, Go, prophesy [give truth] unto my people Israel" (Amos 7:15).

Prophet or Prophetess: an inspired leader who speaks for God; a spokesperson for the Lord. Noah, Moses, and Deborah were all prophets in the Old Testament.

"If there be a prophet [inspired leader] among you, I the Lord will make myself known unto him in a vision" (Numbers 12:6).

Propitiation: the act of appeasing God's wrath. The greatest propitiation occurred when the Atonement of Jesus Christ took place.

"And he is the propitiation [atonement] for our sins" (1 John 2:2).

Prosper: to be successful, thrive, or grow. In the Bible, the term is often used to describe someone who is blessed by God with material or spiritual blessings, like wealth, health, or happiness.

"No weapon that is formed against thee shall prosper [be successful]" (Isaiah 54:17).

Prove: to put to the test, show, or convince. For example, if someone says they are a good artist, they might need to prove it by showing you some of their artwork.

"Examine me, O Lord, and prove me [put me to the test]" (Psalm 26:2).

Proverb: a common saying, words of wisdom, or maxim that gives advice or teaches a lesson. For instance, "A stitch in time saves nine" is a proverb that means if you fix a problem right away, it will prevent bigger problems from happening later.

"Israel shall be a proverb [common saying] and a byword among all people" (1 Kings 9:7).

Provoke: to intentionally or unintentionally cause someone to get angry; or to urge into action. When someone keeps teasing or insulting another person, it might provoke them or cause them to leave the room.

"Beware of him, and obey his voice, provoke him not [don't make him angry]" (Exodus 23:21).

Prudent: to make wise, discerning, or cautious decisions based on common sense or good advice. For example, if you want to buy a new bike, it would be prudent to research which stores sell it for the best price.

"Therefore the prudent [wise] shall keep silence in that time" (Amos 5:13).

Psalm: a form of religious poetry often set to music. The Book of Psalms in the Bible contains many examples of psalms, which were used in Jewish and Christian worship.

"Sing unto him, sing psalms [poetry] unto him, talk ye of all his wondrous works" (1 Chronicles 16:9).

Publican: a Jew who collected tax money for the Romans. Typically, the Publicans were hated and excommunicated. In the New Testament, Matthew was a publican before he was called to be an apostle.

"And all the people that heard him, and the publicans [Jewish tax collectors], justified God, being baptized with the baptism of John" (Luke 7:29).

Publish: to make something known to the public. Before the printing press made publishing common, the act of publishing simply meant to announce or reveal something.

"But he went out, and began to publish [announce] it much" (Mark 1:45).

Puffed Up: to be prideful, or to think too highly of yourself. An example of someone who is puffed up might be a student who boasts about their grades.

"Charity vaunteth not itself, is not puffed up [prideful]" (1 Corinthians 13:4).

Pure: to be clean, clear, or undefiled. For example, if water is pure, it means that it doesn't have any dirt, chemicals, or bacteria in it.

"The commandment of the Lord is pure [clean]" (Psalm 19:8).

Purge: to get rid of something unwanted or harmful, often by washing it or removing it completely. For instance, if someone wants to purge their closet, they might get rid of all the clothes they never wear.

"Whose fan is in his hand, and he will throughly purge [wash] his floor" (Matthew 3:12).

Jesus washing the disciples' feet.

Quake: shaking or trembling of the ground. People can feel quakes as a vibration or a shaking sensation, and it can be a scary and dangerous situation.

"The earth shall quake [shake] before them" (Joel 2:10).

Quarrel: an argument or disagreement between two or more people. Sometimes people in a quarrel may raise their voices, use mean or hurtful words, or even fight physically.

"Forbearing one another, and forgiving one another, if any man have a quarrel [argument] against any" (Colossians 3:13).

Quench: the process of cooling hot metal in water to harden it. If cooled too rapidly, the metal might become to brittle and unusable.

"Thou shalt go no more out with us to battle, that thou quench [cool] not the light of Israel" (2 Samuel 21:17).

Quicken: to make alive, or to resurrect to immortality. For example, when Jesus raised Jairus's daughter from the dead, she was quickened.

"Even when we were dead in sins, hath quickened [resurrect] us together with Christ" (Ephesians 2:5).

Quiver: a case that holds arrows for a bow. A quiver gives an archer quick and easy access to their arrows while keeping them organized and within reach.

"In his quiver [case for arrows] hath he hid me" (Isaiah 49:2).

Rail: to forcefully complain against or scoff at. When a person rails about their job, they are complaining about their work in a loud and aggressive manner. Past tense: railed.

"He wrote also letters to rail on [complain against] the Lord God of Israel" (2 Chronicles 32:17).

Raiment: an old-fashioned word for clothing or fancy garments worn to a wedding. If you hear someone say, "She looked stunning in her raiment," they mean she looked beautiful in her fancy clothes.

"There come in also a poor man in vile raiment [clothes]" (James 2:2).

Raise: to bring up as from childhood, or to rear. Raising a child means providing them with love, care, and support. Raise also sometimes means "to resurrect."

"For, lo, I will raise up [bring up] a shepherd in the land" (Zechariah 11:16).

Ransom: to redeem or buy back; money paid for the release of a prisoner or kidnapped person. Jesus suffered and died as a way to pay the price for the sins of the world, redeeming those who repent.

"I will ransom [redeem] them from the power of the grave" (Hosea 13:14).

Reap: to cut grain with a hook or sickle to gather in a harvest. For example, a farmer might reap a field of wheat when the plants have fully grown, and the grain is ready to be harvested.

"Thou shalt sow, but thou shalt not reap [gather in a harvest]" (Micah 6:15).

Reason: the process of discussing, speaking about, or debating an issue. For example, "I tried to reason with him and explain why his behavior was unacceptable."

"O ye of little faith, why reason [discuss] ye among yourselves" (Matthew 16:8).

Rebuke: to scold someone for errors or faults, usually as a form reprimand or correction. For instance, a teacher might rebuke a student for talking back or disrupting the class.

"I will rebuke [scold] the devourer for your sakes" (Malachi 3:11).

Reckon: to sum up or give an accounting of something. For example, to reckon might involve a person taking responsibility for their actions, especially accounting for money they have spent.

"Howbeit there was no reckoning [accounting] made with them of the money that was delivered into their hand" (2 Kings 22:7).

Recompense: a formal word that means to make up for something by providing its equal. When a person is injured while working, they are usually deserving of recompense in the form of money and time off to heal.

"He shall recompense [make up for] his trespass with the principal thereof" (Numbers 5:7).

Reconcile: to reunite or restore a friendship or a relationship after disagreement or conflict. When two siblings have a fight, their parents might ask them to apologize and reconcile.

"Wherewith should he reconcile [reunite] himself unto his master?" (1 Samuel 29:4).

Redeem: to save a person from sin and spiritual death; also, to rescue or set free. In the Bible, Jesus Christ is the Redeemer because His Atonement saves people from spiritual death.

"But God will redeem [save] my soul from the power of the grave: for he shall receive me" (Psalm 49:15).

Redemption: the act of being delivered or saved from sin. According to the Bible, redemption comes by having faith in Jesus Christ and utilizing the Atonement to repent of our sins.

"For with the Lord there is mercy, and with him is plenteous redemption [deliverance from sin]" (Psalm 130:7).

Reed: tall cane plant that grows along the banks of marshy rivers or streams. Reed plants are often used to make wind instruments, like the clarinet; reed is also the name of an instrument itself.

"What went ye out into the wilderness to see? A reed [tall cane plant] shaken with the wind?" (Matthew 11:7).

Refrain: to control yourself or to hold back from doing something inappropriate. For example, if you were about to say something mean to someone but you decided not to, you refrained.

"Let him refrain [control] his tongue from evil, and his lips that they speak no guile" (1 Peter 3:10).

Refuge: a place of shelter or protection that offers escape from danger. For instance, if someone is in a dangerous situation at home, they might seek refuge at a friend's house.

"The Lord also will be a refuge [shelter] for the oppressed" (Psalm 9:9).

Refuse: to reject, decline or to say no when offered something. For example, if someone offers you a piece of candy but you don't want it, you might refuse by saying, "No, thank you."

"How long refuse [reject] ye to keep my commandments and my laws?" (Exodus 16:28).

Regard: an old-fashioned word that means to glance at or notice something; to consider. When you are regarding the minister at church, you mean you are looking at him.

"Though I fear not God, nor regard [notice] man" (Luke 18:4).

Reign: to rule or have control of the government in a country, like a monarch. During a Queen's reign, she has the power to make laws, establish policies, and control the affairs of the nation.

"The Lord shall reign [rule] for ever and ever" (Exodus 15:18).

Reject: to refuse to accept something, or to set it aside. If someone offers you a solution to a problem, but you don't think it will work, you will likely reject it.

"They have rejected [refused] the word of the Lord" (Jeremiah 8:9).

Rejoice: to feel or show delight, gladness, or happiness. For example, when you finally learn how to ride a bike, you might rejoice by smiling, laughing, and celebrating.

"I rejoice [delight] in thy salvation" (1 Samuel 2:1).

Remain: to stay in the same place or condition without moving or changing. For instance, older children go to school each day, while babies must remain at home.

"They shall perish; but thou remainest [stayed behind]" (Hebrews 1:11).

Remembrance: the act of recalling a memory or recollection. For example, if you look at old photos or talk about memories from a past event, you are engaging in remembrance.

"There is no remembrance [memory] of former things; neither shall there be any remembrance [memory] of things that are to come" (Ecclesiastes 1:11).

Remission of Sins: forgiveness or pardoning of sins through the Atonement of Jesus Christ. When a person is baptized, they are said to receive a remission of their sins.

"And that repentance and remission of sins [forgiveness] should be preached" (Luke 24:47).

Remnant: the remaining part of something that was once larger or complete, particularly of cloth or ribbon. For instance, if you have a piece of cloth left over after making a shirt, it is a remnant of the original fabric.

"The remnant [remaining part] that are left of the captivity there in the province are in great affliction" (Nehemiah 1:3).

Rend or Rent: to tear something apart using force. In Bible times, people would sometimes rend their clothes to show great sorrow.

"And rend [tear] your heart, and not your garments, and turn unto the Lord your God: for he is gracious and merciful, slow to anger, and of great kindness, and repenteth him of the evil" (Joel 2:13).

Repay: to pay back money or a debt owed. If you borrow a dollar from a friend to buy a treat, you will need to repay them the money owed.

"According to their deeds, accordingly he will repay [pay back]" (Isaiah 59:18).

Repentance: feeling regret or sorrow for something that you have done wrong and making a conscious effort to change your behavior or attitude. Repentance is a process made possible by the Atonement of Jesus Christ.

"For godly sorrow worketh repentance [sorrow for sin] to salvation not to be repented [changed] of: but the sorrow of the world worketh death" (2 Corinthians 7:10).

Report: a rumor or gossip about something. For example, a story might be referred to as a "report" even if it had not been verified as true.

"By evil report [rumor] and good report [gossip]" (2 Corinthians 6:8).

Reproach: to express disapproval or shame someone for their behavior. For instance, if you forget to do your homework and your teacher scolds you for it, they are reproaching you.

"Fear ye not the reproach [shame] of men, neither be ye afraid of their revilings" (Isaiah 51:7).

Reproof: when someone blames you for making a mistake, making you feel ashamed. It's like getting a scolding or a lecture for doing something that you shouldn't have done.

"The rod and reproof [blame] give wisdom" (Proverbs 29:15).

Reserve: to keep or something hold back for future use. It's like putting something away in a special place so that you can use it when you need it.

"He hath reserved [kept] in everlasting chains under darkness" (Jude 1:6).

Respect: to have a high or positive opinion of someone or something; to treat well. The Golden Rule, "Treat others as you want to be treated," is a way of showing respect to those around you.

"His eyes shall have respect [high opinion] to the Holy One of Israel" (Isaiah 17:7).

Restitution: compensating to make up for when you've done something wrong or caused harm. For example, if you break your friend's toy, you might buy them a new one as a form of restitution.

"For he should make full restitution [compensation]" (Exodus 22:3).

Restore: to return something to its original condition; to give back to the original owner, or to build up again. When you fix or repair something that was broken, you are restoring it.

"For I will restore [return] health unto thee" (Jeremiah 30:17).

Resurrection: There are two common uses of the word resurrection. Definition 1: specifically, it is event where Jesus rose from the dead after His death and burial in the tomb.

"Jesus said unto her, I am the resurrection [rose from the dead], and the life: he that believeth in me, though he were dead, yet shall he live" (John 11:25).

Definition 2: generally, it is also the reuniting of a person's spirit and body after death, as made possible by Jesus.

"Blessed and holy is he that hath part in the first resurrection [reuniting of body and spirit]" (Revelation 20:6).

Reveal: the process of bringing something out of darkness or obscurity to be visible or exposed. For example, when the curtain is raised in a theater it reveals what was hidden on the stage.

"And the glory of the Lord shall be revealed [made clear]" (Isaiah 40:5).

Reverence: showing deep respect, admiration, and honor towards God; to revere God. Although reverence is a feeling we have, it is usually shown by our actions, including listening attentively, behaving calmly, being polite and respectful, and showing gratitude.

"Wherefore we receiving a kingdom which cannot be moved, let us have grace, whereby we may serve God acceptably with reverence [deep respect] and godly fear" (Hebrews 12:28).

Revile: to attack someone with mean words; to criticize someone harshly. It's like insulting or verbally attacking someone or something with cruel words.

"Who, when he was reviled [criticized], reviled [criticized] not again; when he suffered, he threatened not; but committed himself to him that judgeth righteously" (1 Peter 2:23).

Righteous: being morally right or justifiable by trying to obediently follow God's commandments. Some of the righteous people in the scriptures include Ruth, Peter, and John the Beloved.

"For thou, Lord, wilt bless the righteous [obedient]; with favour wilt thou compass him as with a shield" (Psalm 5:12).

Riotous: to behave in a wild, rowdy, or uncontrolled manner. A riotous person or group can cause a disturbance or uproar that disrupts others around them.

"And there wasted his substance with riotous [wild] living" (Luke 15:13).

Ripe: mature fruit that is ready to be harvested and eaten. For example, a banana is ripe when its color turns from green to yellow.

"Put ye in the sickle, for the harvest is ripe [mature]" (Joel 3:13).

Roar: a deep, loud, continued noise, like the sound of a lion or other wild animals.

"The Lord shall roar [make a loud noise] from on high" (Jeremiah 25:30).

Robe: a part of the temple clothing used in sacred ceremonies. In the Old Testament, the high priests of Israel wore special robes that were adorned with jewels and other decorations. These robes symbolized their priesthood authority.

"And he put upon him the coat, and girded him with the girdle, and clothed him with the robe [temple clothing]" (Leviticus 8:7).

Rod: a long stick or pole. In Bible times, shepherds would use a rod to help guide the sheep.

"Thy rod [stick] and thy staff they comfort me" (Psalm 23:4).

Roll: a scroll or rolled-up piece of parchment or papyrus used anciently as a book. Scrolls were a common way of storing and sharing written texts in the ancient world.

"Take thee a great roll [scroll], and write in it with a man's pen" (Isaiah 8:1).

Root: the base of a plant found under the soil. The roots of a plant help to anchor it into the ground and to absorb water and nutrients from the soil.

"For he shall grow up before him as a tender plant, and as a root [base of a plant] out of a dry ground" (Isaiah 53:2).

Root Out: to find and remove something harmful or dangerous. For example, a gardener might want to root out weeds from the lawn because of their harmful effects.

"And the transgressors shall be rooted out [removed] of it" (Proverbs 2:22).

Rumour: gossip or idle talk, which may not be true or verified. When a friend shares gossip about a classmate supposedly getting in trouble, they are sharing a rumor.

"And ye shall hear of wars and rumours [gossip] of wars" (Matthew 24:6).

Sabbath: a day of rest and worship that is observed by some religions, including Judaism and Christianity. For Christians, the Sabbath is observed on Sundays.

"Let no man therefore judge you in meat, or in drink, or in respect of an holyday, or of the new moon, or of the sabbath [rest] days" (Colossians 2:16).

Sackcloth: clothing made of rough fabric and worn to show grief or sadness. In the Bible, when King David heard that his son Absalom had been killed, he wore sackcloth as a sign of his grief.

"And it came to pass, when king Hezekiah heard it, that he rent his clothes, and covered himself with sackcloth [rough clothing], and went into the house of the Lord" (2 Kings 19:1).

Sacrifice: the act of giving up something valuable or important in order to achieve a greater goal or to show dedication to a cause or belief. In Bible times, the Israelites were commanded to make sacrifices or offerings to God as a form of worship.

"Behold, to obey is better than sacrifice [offer something to God]" (1 Samuel 15:22).

Sadducees: a group of Jewish high priests who were wealthy leaders. The Sadducees were often in disagreement with the Pharisees, another Jewish sect.

"And as they spake unto the people, the priests, and the captain of the temple, and the Sadducees [Jewish leaders], came upon them" (Acts 4:1).

Salvation: the process of being saved from sin and death through Christ's Atonement. Because of the Fall of Adam and Eve, all mankind has fallen, and is in need of salvation by the Savior.

"The Lord is my light and my salvation [Savior]; whom shall I fear? the Lord is the strength of my life; of whom shall I be afraid?" (Psalm 27:1).

Sanctified: the process of being made holy or becoming clean from sin. Sanctification helps us become more like Jesus Christ as we strive to obey His teachings and the promptings of the Holy Ghost.

"By the which will we are sanctified [made holy] through the offering of the body of Jesus Christ once for all" (Hebrews 10:10).

Sanctuary: a sacred or holy place, such as a church, temple, or other place of worship. A sanctuary is often considered a place of spiritual safety or refuge, where people can go to feel closer to their faith.

Elijah and the widow of Zarephath.

"Praise ye the Lord. Praise God in his sanctuary [temple]" (Psalm 150:1).

Scepter: a staff held by a member of royalty. When there is a coronation of a king or queen, they typically hold a scepter to represent justice and authority.

"There shall come a Star out of Jacob, and a Sceptre [staff held by royalty] shall rise out of Israel" (Numbers 24:17).

Scorn: a strong feeling of contempt that causes someone to ridicule others. Scorn can be expressed in many ways, including through words, actions, or facial expressions.

"They laughed us to scorn [contempt], and despised us" (Nehemiah 2:19).

Scourge: a whip or instrument used for punishment or torture, or a person who causes great torment. In the Bible, Jesus was scourged before being crucified.

"They will deliver you up to the councils, and they will scourge [bully] you in their synagogues" (Matthew 10:17).

Scribes: government leaders who also taught the people about the Law of Moses. The scribes were responsible for copying and interpreting the religious texts and were known for being experts in religious law.

"And when the chief priests and scribes [government leaders] saw the wonderful things that he did, . . . they were sore displeased" (Matthew 21:15).

Scrip: an old-fashioned term that refers to a small piece of paper or certificate that was used as money. Scrip was often issued by a company or employer and then used by employees to buy things at company stores.

"Nor scrip [money] for your journey, neither two coats, neither shoes, nor yet staves" (Matthew 10:10).

Sealed: to be bound to God through priesthood power. Being sealed by the Holy Spirit is seen as a sign of God's protection and care of believers.

"Who hath also sealed [bound to God] us, and given the earnest of the Spirit in our hearts" (2 Corinthians 1:22).

Sect: a group of religious people with a specific set of beliefs. A sect usually has beliefs that differ from those of a larger, more mainstream religious or social group.

"But there rose up certain of the sect [group of religious people] of the Pharisees which believed" (Acts 15:5).

Seer: a prophet who can see or perceive things beyond what is visible to the normal eye or can predict future events. In the Bible, Isaiah, Jeremiah, and John the Revelator are all considered to be great seers.

"Come, and let us go to the seer [prophet]: for he that is now called a Prophet was beforetime called a Seer [prophet who sees the future]" (1 Samuel 9:9).

Sepulchre: a tomb or place of burial. In biblical times, sepulchres were typically underground tombs or burial chambers carved into rock.

"And the men of the city told him, It is the sepulchre [tomb] of the man of God, which came from Judah" (2 Kings 23:17).

Shall: a word that is used to show that something will happen in the future, or to express a requirement or obligation. For example, "You shall complete your homework before watching TV" means that completing homework is a requirement or obligation before watching TV.

"Thy Father which seeth in secret shall [will] reward thee openly" (Matthew 6:6).

Shalt: an old-fashioned expression of the word "shall." For instance, "Thou shalt not steal" means "You shall [will] not steal."

"And when thou prayest, thou shalt [will] not be as the hypocrites are" (Matthew 6:5).

Sheaf: a large bundle of grain, typically gathered during harvest, that is tied together. The purpose of tying the grain stalks together is to make them easier to handle and transport. Plural form: sheaves.

"Let her glean even among the sheaves [bundles of grain], and reproach her not" (Ruth 2:15).

Shew: an old-fashioned spelling of the word "show." It means to display something for others to see. If you shew your picture at the art fair, you are displaying it for others to see.

"According to the days of thy coming out of the land of Egypt will I shew [show] unto him marvelous things" (Micah 7:15).

Shod: past tense of the verb "shoe." It means to have fitted or put shoes on someone or something. "I was shod in my new sandals" means that you put on your new sandals.

"And your feet shod [wearing shoes] with the preparation of the gospel of peace" (Ephesians 6:15).

Sickle: a tool with a curved metal blade on a short handle used to harvest grain. To use a sickle, the farmer swings the blade back and forth in a smooth motion, cutting through the stalks of grain near the base.

"Put ye in the sickle [blade], for the harvest is ripe" (Joel 3:13).

Similitude: a word used to describe a comparison, similarity, or likeness between two things. For example, a baby often has a similitude to her parents because she shares certain physical characteristics with them.

"And the similitude [similarity] of the Lord shall he behold" (Numbers 12:8).

Sin: an action or behavior that is morally wrong or against the laws or teachings of God. Lying, stealing, cheating, or hurting others are all examples of different types of sins.

"For the wages of sin [disobedience to God] is death; but the gift of God is eternal life through Jesus Christ our Lord" (Romans 6:23).

Slothful: a person who is lazy or lacks motivation. Someone who is slothful may avoid doing work or physical activity.

"A slothful [lazy] man hideth his hand in his bosom" (Proverbs 19:24).

Smite: to strike, hit, or kill with a heavy blow. In the Bible, the word "smite" is often used to describe God's punishment or anger against sinners. Past tense: smote.

"Smite [strike] a scorner, and the simple will beware: and reprove one that hath understanding, and he will understand knowledge" (Proverbs 19:25).

Solemn: a word that describes something serious, reverent, or dignified. A funeral, for example, is often an event that is described as solemn.

"Upon an instrument of ten strings, and upon the psaltery; upon the harp with a solemn [reverent] sound" (Psalm 92:3).

Sore: the physical sensation of being painful or aching. If a person skins their knee, it will hurt and likely feel sore for several days.

"And, lo, the angel of the Lord came upon them, and the glory of the Lord shone round about them: and they were sore [painfully] afraid" (Luke 2:9).

Statutes: written laws passed by a body of government. In biblical terms, statutes are another way of referring to the commandments or laws of God.

"And that ye may teach the children of Israel all the statutes [commandments] which the Lord hath spoken unto them by the hand of Moses" (Leviticus 10:11).

Stiffnecked: a person who is prideful, hardhearted, or stubborn. A stiffnecked person may be unwilling to consider the new ideas or opinions of others.

"Ye stiffnecked [prideful] and uncircumcised in heart and ears, ye do always resist the Holy Ghost" (Acts 7:51).

Strait: a narrow part or passageway, usually in water or between geographic features. A strait can be difficult to navigate due to its narrowness and the presence of rocks or other hazards.

"Enter ye in at the strait [narrow] gate: for wide is the gate, and broad is the way, that leadeth to destruction, and many there be which go in thereat" (Matthew 7:13).

Strife: a state of conflict, argument, or dispute between people. For example, if two siblings are fighting over a toy, they are experiencing strife.

"Woe is me, my mother, that thou hast borne me a man of strife [argument] and a man of contention to the whole earth!" (Jeremiah 15:10).

Stripe: wounds left after being hit by a whip or rod. In the New Testament, Jesus received stripes when he was whipped before the crucifixion.

"With his stripes [wounds] we are healed" (Isaiah 53:5).

Strive: there are two definitions of strive used in the Bible. Definition 1: to quarrel or argue. If you strive with your sibling over cleaning, you are arguing or having a conflict about cleaning.

"He shall not strive [quarrel], nor cry; neither shall any man hear his voice in the streets" (Matthew 12:19).

Definition 2: to try hard. If you strive to do well on a test in school, you are trying hard to get an A.

"Stand fast in one spirit, with one mind striving [trying hard] together for the faith of the gospel" (Philippians 1:27).

Stubble: short stumps of grain stalks left in the ground after harvest. Stubble on a field is often used as a natural fertilizer because it will decompose and enrich the soil.

"They are as stubble [stumps of grain stalks] before the wind, and as chaff that the storm carrieth away" (Job 21:18).

Subjection: a state of being under the control or authority of someone else. For example, if a person is forced to do something against their will, they might be said to be under subjection.

"Their enemies also oppressed them, and they were brought into subjection [controlled] under their hand" (Psalm 106:42).

Subtilty: the use of clever or devious methods to achieve a goal, such as using subtle manipulation or deceit. If a person cheats, misleads, or betrays, they are using subtilty.

"And consulted that they might take Jesus by subtilty [deceitfulness], and kill him" (Matthew 26:4).

Succour: to give help or aid in a time of great need. For example, a person might provide succor to someone who has lost their home in a natural disaster by offering them food and shelter.

"For in that he himself hath suffered being tempted, he is able to succour [help] them that are tempted" (Hebrews 2:18).

Sufficient: having enough to meet a particular need; an adequate amount. If a student studies enough to get a passing grade on a test, their effort could be considered sufficient.

"Sufficient [there is enough] unto the day is the evil thereof" (Matthew 6:34).

Supplication: the act of humbly asking for help. For example, a person might offer a supplication to God for strength during a difficult time.

"Be careful for nothing; but in every thing by prayer and supplication [humbly asking] with thanksgiving let your requests be made known unto God" (Philippians 4:6).

Sure: a person who is reliable, trustworthy, or confident. If your dad is described as "sure," he is considered dependable.

"The law of the Lord is perfect, converting the soul: the testimony of the Lord is sure [reliable], making wise the simple" (Psalm 19:7).

Sustain: to give support to, or give assistance to, often over a prolonged length of time. For example, if you sustain a friendship, it means that you maintain the friendship over time by staying in touch and supporting each other.

"Yea, forty years didst thou sustain [gave assistance to] them in the wilderness, so that they lacked nothing" (Nehemiah 9:21).

Swaddling Clothes: narrow strips of cloth tightly wrapped around a baby to restrict movement. Newborn babies are often swaddled in blankets to help soothe and comfort them.

"And this shall be a sign unto you; Ye shall find the babe wrapped in swaddling clothes [strips of cloth], lying in a manger" (Luke 2:12).

Swift: the action of moving quickly. When your favorite football player travels swiftly down the field, he is moving quickly.

"Wherefore, my beloved brethren, let every man be swift [quick] to hear, slow to speak, slow to wrath" (James 1:19).

Swine: a pig, hog, or wild boar. Swine are raised for their meat, which is a popular food item around the world.

"Neither cast ye your pearls before swine [pigs], lest they trample them under their feet, and turn again and rend you" (Matthew 7:6).

Synagogue: a place of worship, such as a church or temple. Jewish people call their places of worship synagogues, while Christians tend to use the word church instead.

"For he loveth our nation, and he hath built us a synagogue [place of worship]" (Luke 7:5).

Tabernacle: a portable temple that was moved with the Israelites as they wandered in the wilderness after the Exodus. The Ark of the Covenant was kept in the Tabernacle.

"Then a cloud covered the tent of the congregation, and the glory of the Lord filled the tabernacle [temple]" (Exodus 40:34).

Talent: a unit of measurement for money. Anciently in Attica, Greece a talent was worth about 57.75 lbs. of silver.

"And unto one he gave five talents [pieces of silver], to another two, and to another one; to every man according to his several ability" (Matthew 25:15).

Tares: flowering weeds that grow in wheat fields. Early on, tares look very similar to wheat.

"But while men slept, his enemy came and sowed tares among the wheat, and went his way" (Matthew 13:25).

Tarry: to wait or stay, even if it is time to leave. For example, if you stay after school to help the teacher with a task, you are tarrying.

"Jesus saith unto him, If I will that he tarry [wait] till I come, what is that to thee? follow thou me" (John 21:22).

Temperate: to be self-controlled, reserved, or reasonable in lifestyle choices. A person who declines a second dessert when offered might be considered temperate.

"That the aged men be sober, grave, temperate [reasonable], sound in faith, in charity, in patience" (Titus 2:2).

Tempest: a violent storm with heavy wind and rain. A tempest can be very destructive and dangerous, causing damage to buildings and uprooting trees.

"But the Lord sent out a great wind into the sea, and there was a mighty tempest [storm] in the sea" (Jonah 1:4).

Temple: a religious structure built as a house of the Lord. In the Bible, temples are dedicated to the worship of God. The Savior also used "temple" as a metaphor for the body.

"Thou that destroyest the temple [house of the Lord], and buildest it in three days" (Matthew 27:40).

Tempt: to persuade someone to do something by offering them something appealing or attractive, even if it is not necessarily good for them. The Bible teaches that Satan tempts people to be disobedient to the commandments.

"Considering thyself, lest thou also be tempted [invited to sin]" (Galatians 6:1).

Thee: a word used to refer to someone in a formal or old-fashioned way. Today people use the word "you" instead of "thee." Some use "thee" when praying to show respect to God: "Thank thee for the food we have to eat."

"The Lord bless thee [you], and keep thee [you]" (Numbers 6:24-26).

Thence: an old-fashioned word meaning from that place or from that time. For example, "Thence came all our problems" means from that source came our problems.

"Verily I say unto thee, Thou shalt by no means come out thence [from there], till thou hast paid the uttermost farthing" (Matthew 5:26).

Thine: an old-fashioned word that means "yours." It is used to show possession or ownership of something. For example, "Is this book thine or mine?" While thy is used before a word starting with a consonant, thine is used before a word starting with a vowel or the letter "h."

"And all mine are thine [yours], and thine [yours] are mine; and I am glorified in them" (John 17:10).

Thither: an old-fashioned word meaning there, to that place, or to that direction. Thither is the opposite of hither. It is often used to indicate movement towards a particular location. For example, "He walked from the station and thither to the market."

"And Elijah took his mantle, and wrapped it together, and smote the waters, and they were divided hither and thither [there], so that they two went over on dry ground" (2 Kings 2:8).

Thou: an old-fashioned way of saying "you." It was used as the second person singular pronoun in older forms of English. For example, "Thou art my friend" means "You are my friend."

"Therefore thou art [you are] inexcusable, O man, whosoever thou art [you are] that judgest" (Romans 2:1).

Thy: an old-fashioned way of saying "your." It is used to show possession or ownership of something, like "thy dog" means "your dog." Thy is used before a word starting with a consonant, and thine is used before a word starting with a vowel or the letter "h."

"Jesus said unto him, Thou shalt love the Lord thy [your] God with all thy [your] heart, and with all thy [your] soul, and with all thy [your] mind" (Matthew 22:37-38).

Till: in the Bible till is used in two distinctive ways:
Definition 1: until, or up to a specific point in time or a particular event. The word "till" is a shortened form of the word "until."

"In the sweat of thy face shalt thou eat bread, till [until] thou return unto the ground" (Genesis 3:19).

Definition 2: to prepare the soil for planting crops or seeds. It involves loosening the soil and removing any weeds or other unwanted plants, so the soil is fertile and ready to receive seeds.

"He that tilleth [works] his land shall have plenty of bread: but he that followeth after vain persons shall have poverty enough" (Proverbs 28:19).

Tithe: the practice of giving a portion of one's income or produce to support a church or religious organization. Literally, tithe means a tenth part, so tithing paid is typically 10%.

"And all the tithe [tenth part] of the land, whether of the seed of the land, or of the fruit of the tree, is the Lord's: it is holy unto the Lord" (Leviticus 27:30).

Tittle: a dot or small punctuation mark, such as the dot over a lowercase "i" or "j." In the Bible, Jesus uses the tittle as a metaphor, meaning something small or easily overlooked.

"For verily I say unto you, Till heaven and earth pass, one jot or one tittle [small thing] shall in no wise pass from the law, till all be fulfilled" (Matthew 5:18).

Trespass: a violation of the rights of another person. In biblical teachings, trespass is used more broadly as a description of wrongdoing or sin that is harmful to others.

The Israelites led by a cloud through the wilderness.

"For if ye forgive men their trespasses [wrong doings], your heavenly Father will also forgive you" (Matthew 6:14).

Try: an old-fashioned word that means to test, examine, or to prove. For example, "The manager gave an assignment that would try the employee" means "The manager gave an assignment that would test or prove the employee."

"God left him, to try [test] him" (2 Chronicles 32:31).

Tumult: a loud noise, disturbance, or commotion. For example, a crowd of people shouting and pushing each other in a demonstration would be described as a tumultuous scene.

"And when Eli heard the noise of the crying, he said, What meaneth the noise of this tumult [disturbance]?" (1 Samuel 4:14).

Twain: a word that means two of something or a pair of something. For example, the phrase "two peas in a pod" suggests a twain or pair of peas that are very similar to each other.

"The veil of the temple was rent in twain [two]" (Matthew 27:51).

Unawares: to be caught off guard or surprised by something unexpected. For example, if someone sneaks up behind you and startles you, you might say that they caught you unawares.

"That the slayer might flee thither, which should kill his neighbour unawares [without being aware]" (Deuteronomy 4:42).

Unclean: to state of being sinful, evil, or corrupt. In the Bible we learn that those who are unclean can be made clean through repentance.

"Who can bring a clean thing out of an unclean [sinful]? not one" (Job 14:4).

Unction: the act of anointing someone with oil. For example, when a person is given a blessing for healing, frequently there is first an unction where they are anointed with consecrated oil.

"But ye have an unction [anointing] from the Holy One" (1 John 2:20).

Understanding: to know, be aware of, or to comprehend something. For example, when the teacher reviewed the math problem in class, my understanding of fractions increased.

"Then opened he their understanding [awareness]" (Luke 24:45).

Unfeigned: sincere, genuine, or honest without pretending or trying to deceive. For example, an unfeigned smile is a genuine smile that expresses true happiness or joy.

"I call to remembrance the unfeigned [sincere] faith that is in thee" (2 Timothy 1:5).

Ungodly: something or someone who does not follow God's commandments. According to the Bible, because we all fall short of perfection, everyone except the Savior could be described as ungodly.

"In due time Christ died for the ungodly [the disobedient]" (Romans 5:6).

Unjust: something that is unfair, unreasonable, or sinful according to the laws of God. For example, an unjust person is someone that lies, cheats, or steals from others.

"He that is unjust [sinful], let him be unjust [sinful] still" (Revelation 22:11).

Unworthily: to do something in an unclean manner. For example, if someone behaves unworthily, they are acting in a way that is not in keeping with the commandments of God.

"Whosoever shall eat this bread, and drink this cup of the Lord, unworthily [unclean], shall be guilty" (1 Corinthians 11:27).

Upbraid: to scold, lecture, or criticize for poor behavior. For example, a parent might upbraid a child for misbehaving.

"If any of you lack wisdom, let him ask of God, that giveth to all men liberally, and upbraideth [criticizes] not; and it shall be given him" (James 1:5).

Usurp: to use without permission; to seize or take power or authority without having permission to do so. If someone usurps someone else's authority, they are taking control of a situation that is not rightfully theirs.

"But I suffer not a woman to teach, nor to usurp [take] authority over the man, but to be in silence" (1 Timothy 2:12).

Uttermost: of the greatest or highest amount or degree of something. For example, if someone tries their uttermost, they are putting in their greatest effort or doing everything they possibly can.

"Verily I say unto thee, Thou shalt by no means come out thence, till thou hast paid the uttermost [highest amount] farthing" (Matthew 5:26).

V

Vain: action made without meaning, value, or thought. For example, if a person kisses everyone they meet on the cheek, the gesture is likely impersonal and given in vain.

"Thou shalt not take the name of the Lord thy God in vain [without meaning]" (Exodus 20:7).

Vaunt: to boast or brag about something, especially your own abilities or talents. For example, if someone is vaunting their skills or accomplishments, they are bragging or showing off about them.

"The people that are with thee are too many for me to give the Midianites into their hands, lest Israel vaunt [brag about] themselves against me, saying, Mine own hand hath saved me" (Judges 7:2).

Verily: an old-fashioned word that means in truth, truly, or surely. For example, if someone says "verily, I say unto you", they are emphasizing the truth or certainty of what they are about to say.

"Verily, verily [truthfully], I say unto you, He that entereth not by the door into the sheepfold, but climbeth up some other way, the same is a thief and a robber" (John 10:1).

Vex: to annoy, cause trouble for, or to harass someone. For instance, if a person constantly cracks their knuckles around you, you might feel vexed.

"Thou shalt neither vex [annoy] a stranger, nor oppress him: for ye were strangers in the land of Egypt" (Exodus 22:21).

Vile: something that is sinful, corrupt, or wicked. For example, a jury might find a murder's crime to be so vile that he is sentenced to death.

"For this cause God gave them up unto vile [sinful] affections" (Romans 1:26).

Viper: a type of poisonous snake that has sharp fangs. Although there are many types of vipers, rattlesnakes and adders are two that are well-known.

"And when Paul had gathered a bundle of sticks, and laid them on the fire, there came a viper [snake] out of the heat, and fastened on his hand" (Acts 28:3).

Vow: a promise, oath, or pledge made to show someone is determined to do something. For example, when two people get married, they make a vow to be true to each other.

"Offer unto God thanksgiving; and pay thy vows [promises] unto the most High" (Psalm 50:14).

Wanton: actions that are willful, hard to control, or rude. When a student yells swear words at their teacher and won't follow class rules, their behavior could be described as wanton.

"They have begun to wax wanton against Christ" (1 Timothy 5:11)

Wast: an old-fashioned word for the verb "be" as describing a singular person in the past. When someone says "thou wast," they mean "you were."

"In the day thou wast [were] born thy navel was not cut" (Ezekiel 16:4).

Wavering: to be uncertain or hesitant about a decision or course of action. For example, if someone is wavering between two options, they may be unsure which one to choose, or they may be changing their mind back and forth.

"But let him ask in faith, nothing wavering [hesitant]" (James 1:6).

Wax: to grow in intensity or to expand. For example, with consistent practice and dedication, your muscles will gradually wax [grow] strong and you'll be able to lift heavier weights.

"And my wrath shall wax hot, and I will kill you with the sword" (Exodus 22:24).

Weary: to be physically or mentally exhausted or tired. For instance, if someone has been working long hours and is feeling tired and drained, they might say they are weary.

"Despise not the chastening of the Lord; neither be weary of his correction" (Proverbs 3:11).

Whence: meaning "from where?" It's a way of asking where something came from. For example, you might ask, "Whence did you get that bag?" which means, "Where did you get that bag from?"

"And whence [from where] is this to me, that the mother of my Lord should come to me?" (Luke 1:43).

Wherefore: an old-fashioned word that means why, or for what reason. It's a way of asking for the reason or purpose of something. For example, you might ask, "Wherefore are you crying?" which means, "Why are you crying?"

"Wherefore [for what reason], holy brethren, partakers of the heavenly calling" (Hebrews 3:1).

Wilt: an old-fashioned way of saying will, usually paired as "thou wilt." When someone says, "If thou wilt go to the store, thou wilt need to bring some money." This means "If you will go to the store, you will need to bring some money."

"O Lord, how long shall I cry, and thou wilt [will] not hear!" (Habakkuk 1:2).

Wist: a past tense form of the verb "wit," which means to know or understand. For example, one might say, "I wist not what to do" to mean "I did not know what to do."

"Moses wist [knew] not that the skin of his face shone while he talked with him" (Exodus 34:29).

Woe: a strong expression of grief or anger. For example, a person might say "Woe is me" to express their sorrow or misfortune.

"Woe [anger] unto you, scribes and Pharisees, hypocrites!" (Matthew 23:14).

Word: another name for Christ or His gospel used in the Bible. As The Word, Jesus is the personification of wisdom.

"In the beginning was the Word [Christ], and the Word [Christ] was with God" (John 1:1).

Worship: to show reverence, respect, and devotion towards. Worship frequently occurs at a church and might include singing hymns, scripture reading, taking sacraments, and offering prayers.

"Worship the Lord in the beauty of holiness" (1 Chronicles 16:29).

Worthy: deserving of God's blessings because of obedience to the commandments. In the Bible, worthiness was required to enter God's temple.

"If he will shew himself a worthy [deserving] man, there shall not an hair of him fall to the earth" (1 Kings 1:52).

Wrath: an old-fashioned word that means angry or furious. It's a way of describing someone who is extremely upset and may be showing their anger in a visible way. For example, you might say "He was wroth when he found out that his car had been stolen."

"A soft answer turneth away wrath [anger]" (Proverbs 15:1).

Wrest: to twist or contort something with great effort, manipulation, or force. For instance, if someone tries to wrest control of a company away from its current owners, they are trying to force a takeover.

"Thou shalt not wrest judgment" (Deuteronomy 16:19).

Ye: an old-fashioned way of saying "you." It is the plural form of thou. When a person says "Ye shall know the truth," what they mean is "You shall know the truth."

"How long will ye [you] judge unjustly, and accept the persons of the wicked?" (Psalm 82:2).

Yea: a fancy way of saying "yes." It's often used in formal situations like voting or when people want to show their agreement with something important.

"Yea [yes], thou castest off fear, and restrainest prayer before God" (Job 15:4).

Yearn: to have a deep feeling of desire or wanting something. For example, if you are traveling and feel homesick, you are yearning for home.

"And Joseph made haste; for his bowels did yearn [desired] upon his brother" (Genesis 43:30).

Yield: to give up or surrender to someone or something more powerful. For instance, if you're playing a game of tug-of-war and you let go of the rope, you're yielding to the other team.

"Neither yield [give up] ye your members as instruments of unrighteousness unto sin" (Romans 6:13).

Yoke: a wooden plank that is used to connect two animals, such as oxen, together so that they can pull a heavy load, like a plow or a wagon. The yoke is placed over the animals' necks and is attached to the load they are pulling.

"Take my yoke upon you, and learn of me" (Matthew 11:29).

Yonder: something that is far away but can still be seen or pointed to. For example, if someone points to a mountain range in the distance and says, "Look yonder," they are referring to something that is far away but still visible.

"Remove hence to yonder [far away] place" (Matthew 17:20).

Zeal: a strong feeling of enthusiasm, passion, or devotion towards a particular cause or goal. For example, someone might have a zeal for sports and spend countless hours practicing and competing in their favorite sport.

"And they shall know that I the Lord have spoken it in my zeal [enthusiasm]" (Ezekiel 5:13).

Zealous: to act with intense passion and enthusiasm for a particular cause, activity, or belief. When a person spends a great deal of time, money, and energy on a hobby, they might be described as zealous. "Being more exceedingly zealous [passionate] of the traditions of my fathers" (Galatians 1:14).

Zion: a holy city or a promised land. In the Bible, Jerusalem was sometimes referred to as Zion.

"The Lord hath founded Zion [a holy city]" (Isaiah 14:32).

Other books by Rebecca Irvine:

Let's Learn Together (series of four books)

Improving Family Communication

MTC at Home

Follow the Prophets

Family Home Evening Adventures

Adventures with the Word of God

About Rebecca Irvine

Rebecca Irvine is a graduate of Brigham Young University where she earned both bachelor's and master's degrees in communications. She worked for over 15 years as a marketing research analyst for various ad agencies and PR firms. In addition to a love of writing, Irvine followed in her father's footsteps and became a college professor. She currently teaches communication courses at Benedictine University and Scottsdale Community College. Rebecca is married and the mother of three amazing grown-up kids. Reading, walking, and bingeing Jane Austen films are some of her favorite activities.

Facebook: @Rebecca Irvine
Instagram: @author.RebeccaIrvine

Acknowledgements

Before the baptism of his oldest granddaughter, my brother-in-law Woody went in search of a gift he could give that would help and encourage her to develop the habit of daily scripture study. He had the idea to give her a children's dictionary of common Bible terms. Unfortunately, he couldn't find what he wanted. After his unsuccessful search, he messaged me on Facebook to say I should write it. I readily agreed, thinking it would be a quick and easy concept to put together. It turned out to be more challenging than I initially thought, but the process helped me work on a skill I have wanted to develop (writing for younger readers). So, thank you Woody, for both the idea and helping me to become a better writer!

I also want to thank those who have provided me with feedback along the way. Without this love and support I would never have moved forward. Thank you to my ANWA critique group members for all the advice and support; you're the best! Thank you to Katie for editing assistance and Emily for cover design feedback. And an extra big thank you to my husband Steve for being the best sounding board/thesaurus ever!

Printed in Great Britain
by Amazon